On
Public Speaking and Presenting

HBR's 10 Must Reads series is the definitive collection of ideas and best practices for aspiring and experienced leaders alike. These books offer essential reading selected from the pages of *Harvard Business Review* on topics critical to the success of every manager.

Titles include:

HBR's 10 Must Reads 2015
HBR's 10 Must Reads 2016
HBR's 10 Must Reads 2017
HBR's 10 Must Reads 2018
HBR's 10 Must Reads 2019
HBR's 10 Must Reads 2020
HBR's 10 Must Reads for CEOs
HBR's 10 Must Reads for New Managers
HBR's 10 Must Reads on AI, Analytics, and the New Machine Age
HBR's 10 Must Reads on Boards
HBR's 10 Must Reads on Business Model Innovation
HBR's 10 Must Reads on Change Management
HBR's 10 Must Reads on Collaboration
HBR's 10 Must Reads on Communication
HBR's 10 Must Reads on Design Thinking
HBR's 10 Must Reads on Diversity
HBR's 10 Must Reads on Emotional Intelligence
HBR's 10 Must Reads on Entrepreneurship and Startups
HBR's 10 Must Reads on Innovation
HBR's 10 Must Reads on Leadership
HBR's 10 Must Reads on Leadership, Vol. 2
HBR's 10 Must Reads on Leadership for Healthcare
HBR's 10 Must Reads on Leadership Lessons from Sports
HBR's 10 Must Reads on Making Smart Decisions
HBR's 10 Must Reads on Managing Across Cultures
HBR's 10 Must Reads on Managing in a Downturn
HBR's 10 Must Reads on Managing People

HBR'S
10
MUST
READS

On
Public Speaking and Presenting

HARVARD BUSINESS REVIEW PRESS
Boston, Massachusetts

Library of Congress Cataloging-in-Publication Data

Title: HBR's 10 must reads on public speaking and presenting.
Other titles: Harvard Business Review's ten must reads on public speaking and presenting | HBR's 10 must reads (Series)
Identifiers: LCCN 2019054605 (print) | LCCN 2019054606 (ebook) |
    ISBN 9781633698833 (paperback) | ISBN 9781633698840 (ebook)
Subjects: LCSH: Public speaking. | Business presentations.
Classification: LCC PN4129.15 .H384 2020 (print) | LCC PN4129.15 (ebook) |
    DDC 808.5/1—dc23
LC record available at https://lccn.loc.gov/2019054605
LC ebook record available at https://lccn.loc.gov/2019054606

ISBN: 978-1-63369-883-3
eISBN: 978-1-63369-884-0

Contents

On
**Public
Speaking and
Presenting**

How to Give a Killer Presentation

by Chris Anderson

A LITTLE MORE THAN A YEAR AGO, on a trip to Nairobi, Kenya, some colleagues and I met a 12-year-old Masai boy named Richard Turere, who told us a fascinating story. His family raises livestock on the edge of a vast national park, and one of the biggest challenges is protecting the animals from lions—especially at night. Richard had noticed that placing lamps in a field didn't deter lion attacks, but when he walked the field with a torch, the lions stayed away. From a young age, he'd been interested in electronics, teaching himself by, for example, taking apart his parents' radio. He used that experience to devise a system of lights that would turn on and off in sequence—using solar panels, a car battery, and a motorcycle indicator box—and thereby create a sense of movement that he hoped would scare off the lions. He installed the lights, and the lions stopped attacking. Soon villages elsewhere in Kenya began installing Richard's "lion lights."

The story was inspiring and worthy of the broader audience that our TED conference could offer, but on the surface, Richard seemed an unlikely candidate to give a TED Talk. He was painfully shy. His English was halting. When he tried to describe his invention, the sentences tumbled out incoherently. And frankly, it was hard to imagine a preteenager standing on a stage in front of 1,400 people accustomed to hearing from polished speakers such as Bill Gates, Sir Ken Robinson, and Jill Bolte Taylor.

But Richard's story was so compelling that we invited him to speak. In the months before the 2013 conference, we worked with him to frame his story—to find the right place to begin, and to develop a succinct and logical arc of events. On the back of his invention Richard had won a scholarship to one of Kenya's best schools, and there he had the chance to practice the talk several times in front of a live audience. It was critical that he build his confidence to the point where his personality could shine through. When he finally gave his talk at TED, in Long Beach, you could tell he was nervous, but that only made him more engaging—people were hanging on his every word. The confidence was there, and every time Richard smiled, the audience melted. When he finished, the response was instantaneous: a sustained standing ovation.

Since the first TED conference, 30 years ago, speakers have run the gamut from political figures, musicians, and TV personalities who are completely at ease before a crowd to lesser-known academics, scientists, and writers—some of whom feel deeply uncomfortable giving presentations. Over the years, we've sought to develop a process for helping inexperienced presenters to frame, practice, and deliver talks that people enjoy watching. It typically begins six to nine months before the event, and involves cycles of devising (and revising) a script, repeated rehearsals, and plenty of fine-tuning. We're continually tweaking our approach—because the art of public speaking is evolving in real time—but judging by public response, our basic regimen works well: Since we began putting TED Talks online, in 2006, they've been viewed more than one billion times.

On the basis of this experience, I'm convinced that giving a good talk is highly coachable. In a matter of hours, a speaker's content and delivery can be transformed from muddled to mesmerizing. And while my team's experience has focused on TED's 18-minutes-or-shorter format, the lessons we've learned are surely useful to other presenters—whether it's a CEO doing an IPO road show, a brand manager unveiling a new product, or a start-up pitching to VCs.

Idea in Brief

There are five keys to giving a great presentation:

- Frame your story (figure out where to start and where to end).

- Plan your delivery (decide whether to memorize your speech word for word or develop bullet points and then rehearse it—over and over).

- Work on stage presence (but remember that your story matters more than how you stand or whether you're visibly nervous).

- Plan the multimedia (whatever you do, don't read from Power-Point slides).

- Put it together (play to your strengths and be authentic).

Presentations rise or fall on the quality of the idea, the narrative, and the passion of the speaker. It's about substance—not style. In fact, it's fairly easy to "coach out" the problems in a talk, but there's no way to "coach in" the basic story—the presenter has to have the raw material. So if your thinking is not there yet, decline that invitation to speak. Instead, keep working until you have an idea that's worth sharing.

Frame Your Story

There's no way you can give a good talk unless you have something worth talking about. Conceptualizing and framing what you want to say is the most vital part of preparation.

We all know that humans are wired to listen to stories, and metaphors abound for the narrative structures that work best to engage people. When I think about compelling presentations, I think about taking an audience on a journey. A successful talk is a little miracle—people see the world differently afterward.

If you frame the talk as a journey, the biggest decisions are figuring out where to start and where to end. To find the right place to start, consider what people in the audience already know about your subject—and how much they care about it. If you assume they have more knowledge or interest than they do, or if you start using jargon or get too technical, you'll lose them. The most engaging speakers do a superb job of very quickly introducing the topic, explaining why they care so deeply about it, and convincing the audience members that they should, too.

The biggest problem I see in first drafts of presentations is that they try to cover too much ground. You can't summarize an entire career in a single talk. If you try to cram in everything you know, you won't have time to include key details, and your talk will disappear into abstract language that may make sense if your listeners are familiar with the subject matter but will be completely opaque if they're new to it. You need specific examples to flesh out your ideas. So limit the scope of your talk to that which can be explained, and brought to life with examples, in the available time. Much of the early feedback we give aims to correct the impulse to sweep too broadly. Instead, go deeper. Give more detail. Don't tell us about your entire field of study—tell us about your unique contribution.

Of course, it can be just as damaging to overexplain or painstakingly draw out the implications of a talk. And there the remedy is different: Remember that the people in the audience are intelligent. Let them figure some things out for themselves. Let them draw their own conclusions.

Many of the best talks have a narrative structure that loosely follows a detective story. The speaker starts out by presenting a problem and then describes the search for a solution. There's an "aha" moment, and the audience's perspective shifts in a meaningful way.

If a talk fails, it's almost always because the speaker didn't frame it correctly, misjudged the audience's level of interest, or neglected to tell a story. Even if the topic is important, random pontification without narrative is always deeply unsatisfying. There's no progression, and you don't feel that you're learning.

I was at an energy conference recently where two people—a city mayor and a former governor—gave back-to-back talks. The mayor's talk was essentially a list of impressive projects his city had undertaken. It came off as boasting, like a report card or an advertisement for his reelection. It quickly got boring. When the governor spoke, she didn't list achievements; instead, she shared an idea. Yes, she recounted anecdotes from her time in office, but the idea was

Find the Perfect Mix of Data and Narrative

by Nancy Duarte

MOST PRESENTATIONS LIE SOMEWHERE on the continuum between a report and a story. A report is data-rich, exhaustive, and informative—but not very engaging. Stories help a speaker connect with an audience, but listeners often want facts and information, too. Great presenters layer story and information like a cake, and understand that different types of talks require differing ingredients.

Report
Literal,
informational,
factual,
exhaustive

Story
Dramatic,
experiential,
evocative,
persuasive

Research findings	Financial presentation	Product launch	VC pitch	Keynote address
If your goal is to communicate information from a written report, send the full document to the audience in advance, and limit the presentation to key takeaways. Don't do a long slide show that repeats all your findings. Anyone who's really interested can read the report; everyone else will appreciate brevity.	Financial audiences love data, and they'll want the details. Satisfy their analytical appetite with facts, but add a thread of narrative to appeal to their emotional side. Then present the key takeaways visually, to help them find meaning in the numbers.	Instead of covering only specs and features, focus on the value your product brings to the world. Tell stories that show how real people will use it and why it will change their lives.	For 30 minutes with a VC, prepare a crisp, well-structured story arc that conveys your idea compellingly in 10 minutes or less; then let Q&A drive the rest of the meeting. Anticipate questions and rehearse clear and concise answers.	Formal talks at big events are high-stakes, high-impact opportunities to take your listeners on a transformative journey. Use a clear story framework and aim to engage them emotionally.

central—and the stories explanatory or illustrative (and also funny). It was so much more interesting. The mayor's underlying point seemed to be how great he was, while the governor's message was "Here's a compelling idea that would benefit us all."

As a general rule, people are not very interested in talks about organizations or institutions (unless they're members of them). Ideas and stories fascinate us; organizations bore us—they're much harder to relate to. (Businesspeople especially take note: Don't boast about your company; rather, tell us about the problem you're solving.)

Plan Your Delivery

Once you've got the framing down, it's time to focus on your delivery. There are three main ways to deliver a talk. You can read it directly off a script or a teleprompter. You can develop a set of bullet points that map out what you're going to say in each section rather than scripting the whole thing word for word. Or you can memorize your talk, which entails rehearsing it to the point where you internalize every word—verbatim.

My advice: Don't read it, and don't use a teleprompter. It's usually just too distancing—people will know you're reading. And as soon as they sense it, the way they receive your talk will shift. Suddenly your intimate connection evaporates, and everything feels a lot more formal. We generally outlaw reading approaches of any kind at TED, though we made an exception a few years ago for a man who insisted on using a monitor. We set up a screen at the back of the auditorium, in the hope that the audience wouldn't notice it. At first he spoke naturally. But soon he stiffened up, and you could see this horrible sinking feeling pass through the audience as people realized, "Oh, no, he's reading to us!" The words were great, but the talk got poor ratings.

Many of our best and most popular TED Talks have been memorized word for word. If you're giving an important talk and you have the time to do this, it's the best way to go. But don't underestimate the work involved. One of our most memorable speakers was Jill Bolte Taylor, a brain researcher who had suffered a stroke. She talked about what she learned during the eight years it took her to recover. After crafting her story and undertaking many hours of solo practice, she rehearsed her talk dozens of times in front of an audience to be sure she had it down.

Obviously, not every presentation is worth that kind of investment of time. But if you do decide to memorize your talk, be aware that there's a predictable arc to the learning curve. Most people go through what I call the "valley of awkwardness," where they haven't quite memorized the talk. If they give the talk while stuck in that valley, the audience will sense it. Their words will sound recited, or there will be painful moments where they stare into the middle distance, or cast their eyes upward, as they struggle to remember their lines. This creates distance between the speaker and the audience.

Getting past this point is simple, fortunately. It's just a matter of rehearsing enough times that the flow of words becomes second nature. Then you can focus on delivering the talk with meaning and authenticity. Don't worry—you'll get there.

But if you don't have time to learn a speech thoroughly and get past that awkward valley, don't try. Go with bullet points on note cards. As long as you know what you want to say for each one, you'll be fine. Focus on remembering the transitions from one bullet point to the next.

Also pay attention to your tone. Some speakers may want to come across as authoritative or wise or powerful or passionate, but it's usually much better to just sound conversational. Don't force it. Don't orate. Just be you.

If a successful talk is a journey, make sure you don't start to annoy your travel companions along the way. Some speakers project too much ego. They sound condescending or full of themselves, and the audience shuts down. Don't let that happen.

Develop Stage Presence

For inexperienced speakers, the physical act of being onstage can be the most difficult part of giving a presentation—but people tend to overestimate its importance. Getting the words, story, and substance right is a much bigger determinant of success or failure than how

How to Stop Saying "Um," "Ah," and "You Know"

by Noah Zandan

Um.

Ah.

So.

You know.

Like.

Right?

Well.

WHEN WE FIND OURSELVES RATTLED while speaking—whether we're nervous, distracted, or at a loss for what comes next—it's easy to lean on filler words. These may give us a moment to collect our thoughts before we press on, and in some cases, they may be useful indicators that the audience should pay special attention to what we're about to say. But when we start to overuse them, they become verbal crutches that diminish our credibility and distract from our message.

The good news is that you can turn this weakness into a strength by replacing filler words with pauses.

Research suggests that most conversational speech consists of short (0.20 second), medium (0.60 second), and long (over 1 second) pauses. Great public speakers often pause for two to three seconds or even longer. My firm's phonetic data shows that the average speaker uses only 3.5 pauses per minute, and that's not enough.

you stand or whether you're visibly nervous. And when it comes to stage presence, a little coaching can go a long way.

The biggest mistake we see in early rehearsals is that people move their bodies too much. They sway from side to side, or shift their weight from one leg to the other. People do this naturally when they're nervous, but it's distracting and makes the speaker seem weak. Simply getting a person to keep his or her lower body motionless can dramatically improve stage presence. There are some people

This is understandable. For many speakers, even the briefest pause can feel like an interminable silence. That's because we tend to think faster than we speak.

Despite how they might feel at first, well-placed pauses make you sound calm and collected, and they help you gather your thoughts, calm your nerves, and build suspense.

The first step in changing any habit is awareness. To identify your crutch words, watch the video or review the transcript of your most recent talk, and determine what vocal fillers you rely on most. Once you're aware of them, you'll likely start to hear yourself say these words in your day-to-day communication. Pair your crutch words with actions. So for instance, every time you catch yourself saying "like," tap your leg. Or have a family member or close friend monitor a practice session and bring your attention to your crutch words with a clap or a finger snap.

Next, begin forcing yourself to be silent. To practice, record yourself on video talking about what you did from the beginning to the end of the day. Rehearse using pauses instead of filler words as you recall the events.

Finally, I can't stress enough the importance of preparation. Nervousness is one of the biggest reasons people overuse vocal fillers. The less prepared you are, the more nervous you'll be, which will likely cause you to speak too quickly, trip over your words, or forget what's next. So practice. On average, the optimal ratio of preparation to performance is one hour of practice for every minute of performance. This might sound like a lot, but Trey Guinn, a professor of communications at the University of Texas at Austin, recommends speakers get in at least three trial runs before stepping in front of an audience.

who are able to walk around a stage during a presentation, and that's fine if it comes naturally. But the vast majority are better off standing still and relying on hand gestures for emphasis.

Perhaps the most important physical act onstage is making eye contact. Find five or six friendly looking people in different parts of the audience and look them in the eye as you speak. Think of them as friends you haven't seen in a year, whom you're bringing up to date on your work. That eye contact is incredibly powerful, and it will do more than anything else to help your talk land. Even if you don't have time to prepare fully and have to read from a script, looking up and making eye contact will make a huge difference.

Another big hurdle for inexperienced speakers is nervousness—both in advance of the talk and while they're onstage. People deal with this in different ways. Many speakers stay out in the audience until the moment they go on; this can work well, because keeping your mind engaged in the earlier speakers can distract you and limit nervousness. Amy Cuddy, a Harvard Business School professor who studies how certain body poses can affect power, utilized one of the more unusual preparation techniques I've seen. She recommends that people spend time before a talk striding around, standing tall, and extending their bodies; these poses make you feel more powerful. It's what she did before going onstage, and she delivered a phenomenal talk. But I think the single best advice is simply to breathe deeply before you go onstage. It works.

In general, people worry too much about nervousness. Nerves are not a disaster. The audience *expects* you to be nervous. It's a natural body response that can actually improve your performance: It gives you energy to perform and keeps your mind sharp. Just keep breathing, and you'll be fine.

Acknowledging nervousness can also create engagement. Showing your vulnerability, whether through nerves or tone of voice, is one of the most powerful ways to win over an audience, provided it is authentic. Susan Cain, who wrote a book about introverts and spoke at our 2012 conference, was terrified about giving her talk. You could feel her fragility onstage, and it created this dynamic where the audience was rooting for her—everybody wanted to hug her afterward. The fact that we knew she was fighting to keep herself up there made it beautiful, and it was the most popular talk that year.

Plan the Multimedia

With so much technology at our disposal, it may feel almost mandatory to use, at a minimum, presentation slides. By now most people have heard the advice about PowerPoint: Keep it simple; don't use a slide deck as a substitute for notes (by, say, listing the bullet points you'll discuss—those are best put on note cards); and don't repeat out loud words that are on the slide. Not only is reciting slides a variation of the teleprompter problem—"Oh, no, she's reading to us, too!"—but information is interesting only once, and hearing and seeing the same words feels repetitive. That advice may seem universal by now, but go into any company and you'll see presenters violating it every day.

Many of the best TED speakers don't use slides at all, and many talks don't require them. If you have photographs or illustrations that make the topic come alive, then yes, show them. If not, consider doing without, at least for some parts of the presentation. And if you're going to use slides, it's worth exploring alternatives to PowerPoint. For instance, TED has invested in the company Prezi, which makes presentation software that offers a camera's-eye view of a two-dimensional landscape. Instead of a flat sequence of images, you can move around the landscape and zoom in to it if need be. Used properly, such techniques can dramatically boost the visual punch of a talk and enhance its meaning.

Artists, architects, photographers, and designers have the best opportunity to use visuals. Slides can help frame and pace a talk and help speakers avoid getting lost in jargon or overly intellectual language. (Art can be hard to talk about—better to experience it visually.) I've seen great presentations in which the artist or designer put slides on an automatic timer so that the image changed every 15 seconds. I've also seen presenters give a talk accompanied by video, speaking along to it. That can help sustain momentum. The industrial designer Ross Lovegrove's highly visual TED Talk, for instance, used this technique to bring the audience along on a remarkable creative journey.

Another approach creative types might consider is to build silence into their talks, and just let the work speak for itself. The kinetic sculptor Reuben Margolin used that approach to powerful effect. The idea is not to think "I'm giving a talk." Instead, think "I want to give this audience a powerful experience of my work." The single worst thing artists and architects can do is to retreat into abstract or conceptual language.

Video has obvious uses for many speakers. In a TED Talk about the intelligence of crows, for instance, the scientist showed a clip of a crow bending a hook to fish a piece of food out of a tube—essentially creating a tool. It illustrated his point far better than anything he could have said.

Used well, video can be very effective, but there are common mistakes that should be avoided. A clip needs to be short—if it's more than 60 seconds, you risk losing people. Don't use videos— particularly corporate ones—that sound self-promotional or like infomercials; people are conditioned to tune those out. Anything with a soundtrack can be dangerously off-putting. And whatever you do, don't show a clip of yourself being interviewed on, say, CNN. I've seen speakers do this, and it's a really bad idea—no one wants to go along with you on your ego trip. The people in your audience are already listening to you live; why would they want to simultaneously watch your talking-head clip on a screen?

Putting It Together

We start helping speakers prepare their talks six months (or more) in advance so that they'll have plenty of time to practice. We want people's talks to be in final form at least a month before the event. The more practice they can do in the final weeks, the better off they'll be. Ideally, they'll practice the talk on their own and in front of an audience.

The tricky part about rehearsing a presentation in front of other people is that they will feel obligated to offer feedback and constructive criticism. Often the feedback from different people will vary or directly conflict. This can be confusing or even paralyzing, which is why it's important to be choosy about the people you use as a test audience, and whom you invite to offer feedback. In general, the more experience a person has as a presenter, the better the criticism he or she can offer.

I learned many of these lessons myself in 2011. My colleague Bruno Giussani, who curates our TEDGlobal event, pointed out that although I'd worked at TED for nine years, served as the emcee at our

10 Ways to Ruin a Presentation

AS HARD AS IT MAY BE to give a great talk, it's really easy to blow it. Here are some common mistakes that TED advises its speakers to avoid.

1. Take a really long time to explain what your talk is about.
2. Speak slowly and dramatically. Why talk when you can orate?
3. Make sure you subtly let everyone know how important you are.
4. Refer to your book repeatedly. Even better, quote yourself from it.
5. Cram your slides with numerous text bullet points and multiple fonts.
6. Use lots of unexplained technical jargon to make yourself sound smart.
7. Speak at great length about the history of your organization and its glorious achievements.
8. Don't bother rehearsing to check how long your talk is running.
9. Sound as if you're reciting your talk from memory.
10. Never, ever make eye contact with anyone in the audience.

conferences, and introduced many of the speakers, I'd never actually given a TED Talk myself. So he invited me to give one, and I accepted.

It was more stressful than I'd expected. Even though I spend time helping others frame their stories, framing my own in a way that felt compelling was difficult. I decided to memorize my presentation, which was about how web video powers global innovation, and that was really hard: Even though I was putting in a lot of hours, and getting sound advice from my colleagues, I definitely hit a point where I didn't quite have it down and began to doubt I ever would. I really thought I might bomb. I was nervous right up until the moment I took the stage. But it ended up going fine. It's definitely not one of the all-time great TED Talks, but it got a positive reaction—and I survived the stress of going through it.

Ultimately I learned firsthand what our speakers have been discovering for three decades: Presentations rise or fall on the quality of the idea, the narrative, and the passion of the speaker. It's about substance, not speaking style or multimedia pyrotechnics. It's fairly easy to "coach out" the problems in a talk, but there's no way to "coach in" the basic story—the presenter has to have the raw material. If you have something to say, you can build a great talk. But if the central theme isn't there, you're better off not speaking. Decline the invitation. Go back to work, and wait until you have a compelling idea that's really worth sharing.

The single most important thing to remember is that there is no one good way to do a talk. The most memorable talks offer something fresh, something no one has seen before. The worst ones are those that feel formulaic. So do not on any account try to emulate every piece of advice I've offered here. Take the bulk of it on board, sure. But make the talk your own. You know what's distinctive about you and your idea. Play to your strengths and give a talk that is truly authentic to you.

Originally published in June 2013. Reprint R1306K

How to Become an Authentic Speaker

by Nick Morgan

AT A COMPANYWIDE SALES MEETING, Carol, a vice president of sales, strides energetically to the podium, pauses for a few seconds to look at the audience, and then tells a story from her days as a field rep. She deftly segues from her anecdote to a positive assessment of the company's sales outlook for the year, supplementing her speech with colorful slides showing strong growth and exciting new products in the pipeline. While describing those products, she accents her words with animated gestures.

Having rehearsed carefully in front of a small audience of trusted colleagues, all of whom liked her message and her energy, she now confidently delivers the closer: Walking to the edge of the stage, she scans the room and challenges her listeners to commit to a stretch sales goal that will put many of them in the annual winners' circle.

But Carol senses that something's amiss. The audience isn't exhibiting the kind of enthusiasm needed to get the year off to a great start. She begins to panic: What's happening? Is there anything she can do to salvage the situation?

We all know a Carol. (You may be one yourself.) We've all heard speeches like hers, presentations in which the speaker is apparently doing all the right things, yet something—something we can't quite identify—is wrong.

If asked about these speeches, we might describe them as "calculated," "insincere," "not real," or "phoned in." We probably wouldn't be able to say exactly why the performance wasn't compelling. The speaker just didn't seem *authentic*.

In today's difficult economy, and especially in the aftermath of numerous scandals involving individual executives, employees and shareholders are more skeptical than ever. Authenticity—including the ability to communicate authentically with others—has become an important leadership attribute. When leaders have it, they can inspire their followers to make extraordinary efforts on behalf of their organizations. When they don't, cynicism prevails and few employees do more than the minimum necessary to get by.

In my 22 years of working as a communications coach, I have seen again and again how hard it is for managers to come across in public communications as authentic—even when they passionately believe their message. Why is this kind of communication so difficult? Why can't people just stand up and tell the truth?

What Science Teaches Us

The answer lies in recent research into the ways our brains perceive and process communication. We all know by now the power of nonverbal communication—what I call the "second conversation." If your spoken message and your body language are mismatched, audiences will respond to the nonverbal message every time. Gestures speak louder than words. And that means you *can't* just stand up and tell the truth. You'll often hear someone say in advance of a speech, "I don't want to look over-rehearsed, so I'm going to wing it." But during the presentation his body language will undermine his credibility. Because he's in a stressful situation with no preparation, he'll appear off-kilter. Whatever the message of his words, he'll seem to be learning as he goes—not likely to engender confidence in a leader.

So preparation is important. But the traditional approach—careful rehearsal like Carol's—often doesn't work either. That's because it usually involves specific coaching on nonverbal elements—"maintain eye contact," "spread your arms," "walk out from behind the podium"—that can ultimately make the speaker seem artificial. The audience can see the wheels turning in her head as she goes through the motions.

Idea in Brief

You rehearsed your speech thoroughly—and mastered that all-important body language. But when you delivered the talk, you sensed little enthusiasm in your audience.

What's going on? You're probably coming across as artificial. The reason: When we rehearse specific body language elements, we use them incorrectly during the actual speech—slightly *after* speaking the associated words. Listeners feel something's wrong, because during natural conversation, body language emerges *before* the associated words.

To demonstrate your authenticity, don't rehearse your body language. Instead, imagine meeting four aims:

- Being open to your audience
- Connecting with your audience
- Being passionate about your topic
- Listening to your audience

When you rehearse this way, you'll genuinely experience these feelings when delivering your speech. Your body language will emerge at the right moment. And your listeners will know you're the real thing.

Why does this calculated body language come off as inauthentic? Here's where the brain research comes in. We're learning that in human beings the second, nonverbal conversation actually starts *first,* in the instant after an emotion or an impulse fires deep within the brain but before it has been articulated. Indeed, research shows that people's natural and unstudied gestures are often indicators of what they will think and say next.

You might say that words are after-the-fact explanations of why we just gestured as we did. Think of something as simple as a hug: The impulse to embrace someone begins *before* the thought that you're glad to see him or her has fully formed, much less been expressed aloud. Or think about a typical conversation: Reinforcement, contradiction, and commentary arise first in gesture. We nod vigorously, shake our heads, roll our eyes, all of which express our reactions more immediately—and more powerfully—than words can.

If gesture precedes conscious thought and thought precedes words—even if by no more than a tiny fraction of a second—that changes our thinking about speech preparation. When coached in the traditional way, rehearsing specific gestures one by one, speakers

Idea in Practice

Morgan recommends rehearsing your speeches with these four aims in mind.

Being open to your audience

To rehearse being open, practice your speech by envisioning what it would be like to give your presentation to someone you're completely comfortable with. The person could be your spouse, a close friend, or your child. Notice especially what this feels like: This is the emotional state you want to be in when you deliver the speech.

This state leads to more natural body language, such as smiles and relaxed shoulders. And the behaviors in turn lead to more candid expression of your thoughts and feelings.

Connecting with your audience

As you practice your speech, think about wanting to engage with your listeners. Imagine that a young child you know well isn't heeding you. You want to capture—and keep—his attention however you can.

In such situations, you don't strategize; you simply do what feels natural and appropriate. For example, you increase the intensity or volume of your voice or move closer to your listener. During your actual speech, these behaviors will happen naturally and with the right timing.

end up employing those gestures at the same time that—or even slightly after—they speak the associated words. Although audiences are not consciously aware of this unnatural sequence, their innate ability to read body language leads them to feel that something's wrong—that the speaker is inauthentic.

"Rehearsing" Authenticity

So if neither casual spontaneity nor traditional rehearsal leads to compelling communication, how can you prepare for an important presentation? You have to tap into the basic impulses underlying your speech. These should include four powerful aims: to be open, to connect, to be passionate, and to listen. Each of these aims informs nearly all successful presentations.

Rehearse your speech with them in mind. Try practicing it four ways, adopting the mind-set of each aim in turn, feeling it more than thinking about it. Forget about rehearsing specific gestures. If you are able to sin-

Being passionate about your topic

While rehearsing, ask yourself what in your topic you feel deeply about: What's at stake? What results do you want your presentation to produce? Focus not on what you want to say but on why you're giving the speech and how you feel about it. Let the underlying emotion come out in every word you deliver during rehearsal. You'll infuse the actual speech with some of that passion and come across as more human and engaging.

"Listening" to your audience

To practice fulfilling this aim, think about what your listeners will likely be feeling when you step up to begin your presentation. Are they excited about the future? Worried about bad news? As you practice, imagine watching them closely, looking for signs of their response to you.

During your presentation, you'll be more prepared to identify the emotions your listeners are sending to you via nonverbal means. And you'll be able to respond to them appropriately; for example, by picking up the pace, varying your language, asking an impromptu question, or even eliminating or changing parts of your talk.

cerely realize these feelings, your body language will take care of itself, emerging naturally and at the right moment. (The approach described here may also lead you to refine some of your verbal message, to make it accord with your nonverbal one.) When you actually deliver the speech, continue to focus on the four underlying aims.

Note the paradox here. This method is designed to achieve authenticity through the mastery of a calculated process. But authenticity arises from the four aims, or what I call "intents," that I have mentioned. If you can physically and emotionally embody all four, you'll achieve the perceived *and* real authenticity that creates a powerful bond with listeners.

What Underlies an Authentic Speech

Creating that bond isn't easy. Let me offer some advice for tapping into each of the four intents.

A Speech Is Not an Essay

by John Coleman

FOR THOSE NEW TO PUBLIC SPEAKING, the tendency to mimic the forms and features of writing can be crippling.

The average adult reads 300 words per minute, but people can only follow speech closely at around 150 to 160 words per minute. Similarly, studies have shown that auditory memory is inferior to visual memory, and while most of us can read for hours, our ability to focus on a speech is more constrained. It's important, then, to write brief and clear speeches. Ten minutes of speaking is only about 1,300 words, and while written texts—which can be reviewed, studied, and reexamined—can be subtle and nuanced, the spoken word is followed in the moment and must be appropriately short, sweet, and to the point.

It's also important to signpost and review key points within your speech. In a written essay, readers can revisit confusing passages or missed points. But once you lose someone in a speech, that person may be lost for good. In your introduction, state your thesis and then lay out the structure of your speech (e.g., "We'll see this in three ways: x, y, and z"). Then open each new point with a signpost to orient your listeners, with words such as "to begin," "secondly," and "finally," and close each point with a similar signpost (e.g., "So

The intent to be open with your audience

This is the first and in some ways the most important thing to focus on in rehearsing a speech, because if you come across as closed, your listeners will perceive you as defensive—as if they somehow represent a threat. Not much chance for communication there.

How can you become more open? Try to imagine giving your presentation to someone with whom you're completely relaxed—your spouse, a close friend, your child. Notice what that mental picture looks like but particularly what it *feels* like. This is the state you need to be in if you are to have an authentic rapport with your audience.

If it's hard to create this mental image, try the real thing. Find a patient friend and push yourself to be open with him or her. Notice what that scene looks like and, again, how you feel. Don't overintellectualize: This is a bit like practicing a golf swing or a tennis serve. Although you might make tiny mental notes about what you're

we now see, the first element of success is x"). This lack of subtlety would be repetitive and inelegant in a written document, but it is essential to a speech.

Similarly, the subtleties of complex argumentation and statistical analysis can be compelling in an essay, but in a speech you should keep the statistics to a minimum and opt for longer and more vivid stories. Lead or end an important point with the relevant statistics. But never fall into reciting strings of numbers or citations.

And remember that when you're speaking, your audience doesn't have the benefit of commas, quotation marks, paragraph breaks, or exclamation points. Instead, use your voice, your hand gestures, your pace, and even your posture and position on stage to give your speech texture and range. Vary your level of excitement, your tone, and your volume for emphasis. Use hand gestures consciously and in keeping with the points you're trying to make. Between main points, walk to another spot on the stage to indicate that a new part of your presentation is beginning.

If you're a great writer, don't assume that talent will translate to the spoken word. "A speech is not an essay on its hind legs," as communications professor Bob Frank says, and great speech writers and public speakers adapt accordingly.

doing, they shouldn't get in the way of recognizing a feeling that you can try to replicate later.

Openness immediately feels risky to many people. I worked with a CEO who was passionate about his work, but his audiences didn't respond. He realized that he'd learned as a boy not to show emotion precisely about the things that meant the most to him. We had to replace this felt experience with one of talking to a close friend he was excited to see.

Let's go back to Carol (a composite of several clients). As she works on feeling more open in her presentations, her face begins to light up with a big smile when she speaks, and her shoulders relax. She realizes that without meaning to, she has come across as so serious that she has alienated her audiences.

A change in nonverbal behavior can affect the spoken message. Over and over, I've seen clients begin speaking more comfortably—and more authentically—as the intent to be more open physically led to a more candid expression of their thoughts.

The intent to connect with your audience

Once you begin to feel open, and you've stored away the memory of what it looks and feels like, you're ready to practice the speech again, this time focusing on the audience. Think about wanting—*needing*—to engage your listeners. Imagine that a young child you know well isn't heeding you. You want to capture that child's attention however you can. You don't strategize—you simply do what feels natural and appropriate. You increase the intensity or volume of your voice or move closer.

You also want to *keep* your audience's attention. Don't let listeners slide away into their thoughts instead of following yours. Here, you might transform your young child into a teenager and imagine yearning to keep this easily distractible listener focused on your words.

If openness is the ante that lets you into the game, connection is what keeps the audience playing. Now that Carol is intent on being connected with her listeners, she realizes that she typically waits too long—in fact, until the very end of her speech—to make contact with them. She begins her next presentation by reaching out to audience members who have contributed significantly to the company's sales success, establishing a connection that continues throughout her speech.

The intent to be passionate about your topic

Ask yourself what it is that you feel deeply about. What's at stake? What results do you want your presentation to produce? Are you excited about the prospects of your company? Worried that they look bleak? Determined to improve them?

Focus not on what you want to say but on why you're giving the speech and how you feel about that. Let the underlying emotion come out (once you've identified it, you won't need to force it) in every word you deliver during this round of rehearsal. Then raise the stakes for yourself: Imagine that somebody in the audience has the power to take everything away from you unless you win him or her over with your passionate argument.

I worked with a senior partner at a consulting firm who was planning to talk to her colleagues about the things at the firm she valued and wanted to pass on to the next generation as she got ready to retire. Her speech, when she began practicing it, was a crystal-clear but dull commentary on the importance of commitment and hard work. As she began focusing on the emotion beneath the speech, she recalled how her mother, a dancer, had instilled in her the value of persisting no matter what the obstacles. She decided to acknowledge her mother in her talk. She said that her mother, then 92, had never let the pain and difficulties she had experienced during her career obscure her joy in performing. Although the speaker shed most of her tears during rehearsal, her passion transformed the talk into something memorable.

Somewhat more prosaically, Carol begins to think about what she's passionate about—her determination to beat a close competitor—and how that might inform her presentations. She realizes that this passion fuels her energy and excitement about her job. She infuses her next speech with some of that passion and immediately comes across as more human and engaging.

The intent to "listen" to your audience

Now begin thinking about what your listeners are likely to be feeling when you step up to begin your presentation. Are they excited about the future? Worried about bad sales news? Hopeful they can keep their jobs after the merger? As you practice, imagine yourself watching them very closely, looking for signs of their response to you.

Of course, your intent to discover the audience's emotional state will be most important during the actual presentation. Usually your listeners won't actually be talking to you, but they will be sending you nonverbal messages that you'll need to pick up and respond to.

This isn't as hard as it may sound. As a fellow member of the human race, you are as expert as your audience in reading body language—if you have an intent to do so. As you read the messages your listeners are sending with their bodies, you may want to pick up the pace, vary your language, even change or eliminate parts of your talk. If this leads you to involve the audience in a real dialogue—say, by asking an impromptu question—so much the better.

If time has been set aside for questions at the end of your presentation, you'll want to listen to the audience with your whole body, keeping yourself physically and psychologically still in the way you might when someone is telling you something so important that you dare not miss a word. Without thinking about it, you'll find yourself leaning forward or nodding your head—gestures that would appear unnatural if you were doing them because you'd been told to.

Of course, listening to and responding to an audience in the middle of your speech requires that you have your material down cold. But you can also take what your listeners tell you and use it to improve future presentations. I worked with a sales executive who had been so successful that she began touring the world in order to share her secrets with others. In listening to audiences, paying attention to their bodies as well as their words, she began to realize that they didn't just want to receive what she had to say; they wanted to give her something in return. The executive's speeches were inspiring, and her listeners wanted to thank her. So we designed a brief but meaningful ceremony near the end of her speech that allowed the audience members to get up, interact with one another, and give back to the speaker some of the inspiration she was giving them.

Consider Carol once again. Because of her intent to pick up on her listeners' emotions, Carol begins to realize over the course of several speeches that she has been wrongly assuming that her salespeople share her sense of urgency about their major competitor. She resolves to spend more time at the beginning of her next presentation explaining why stretch goals are important. This response to her listeners' state of mind, when combined with her own desire to be open, connected, and passionate, strengthens her growing ability to come across as—and be—an authentic speaker.

Originally published in November 2008. Reprint R0811H

Storytelling
That Moves People

A Conversation with Screenwriting Coach
Robert McKee. *by Bronwyn Fryer*

PERSUASION IS THE CENTERPIECE of business activity. Customers must be convinced to buy your company's products or services, employees and colleagues to go along with a new strategic plan or reorganization, investors to buy (or not to sell) your stock, and partners to sign the next deal. But despite the critical importance of persuasion, most executives struggle to communicate, let alone inspire. Too often, they get lost in the accoutrements of company-speak: PowerPoint slides, dry memos, and hyperbolic missives from the corporate communications department. Even the most carefully researched and considered efforts are routinely greeted with cynicism, lassitude, or outright dismissal.

Why is persuasion so difficult, and what can you do to set people on fire? In search of answers to those questions, HBR senior editor Bronwyn Fryer paid a visit to Robert McKee, the world's best-known and most respected screenwriting lecturer, at his home in Los Angeles. An award-winning writer and director, McKee moved to California after studying for his Ph.D. in cinema arts at the University of Michigan. He then taught at the University of Southern California's School of Cinema and Television before forming his own company, Two-Arts, to take his lectures on the art of storytelling worldwide to an audience of writers, directors, producers, actors, and entertainment executives.

McKee's students have written, directed, and produced hundreds of hit films, including *Forrest Gump, Erin Brockovich, The Color Purple, Gandhi, Monty Python and the Holy Grail, Sleepless in Seattle, Toy Story,* and *Nixon.* They have won 18 Academy Awards, 109 Emmy Awards, 19 Writers Guild Awards, and 16 Directors Guild of America Awards. Emmy Award winner Brian Cox portrays McKee in the 2002 film *Adaptation,* which follows the life of a screenwriter trying to adapt the book *The Orchid Thief.* McKee also serves as a project consultant to film and television production companies such as Disney, Pixar, and Paramount as well as major corporations, including Microsoft, which regularly send their entire creative staffs to his lectures.

McKee believes that executives can engage listeners on a whole new level if they toss their PowerPoint slides and learn to tell good stories instead. In his best-selling book *Story: Substance, Structure, Style, and the Principles of Screenwriting,* published in 1997 by Harper-Collins, McKee argues that stories "fulfill a profound human need to grasp the patterns of living—not merely as an intellectual exercise, but within a very personal, emotional experience." What follows is an edited and abridged transcript of McKee's conversation with HBR.

Why should a CEO or a manager pay attention to a screenwriter?

A big part of a CEO's job is to motivate people to reach certain goals. To do that, he or she must engage their emotions, and the key to their hearts is story. There are two ways to persuade people. The first is by using conventional rhetoric, which is what most executives are trained in. It's an intellectual process, and in the business world it usually consists of a PowerPoint slide presentation in which you say, "Here is our company's biggest challenge, and here is what we need to do to prosper." And you build your case by giving statistics and facts and quotes from authorities. But there are two problems with rhetoric. First, the people you're talking to have their own set of authorities, statistics, and experiences. While you're trying to persuade them, they are arguing with you in their heads. Second, if you do succeed in persuading them, you've done so only on an intellectual basis. That's not good enough, because people are not inspired to act by reason alone.

Idea in Brief

As human beings, we make sense of our experiences through stories. But becoming a good storyteller is hard. It requires imagination and an understanding of what makes a story worth telling. All great stories deal with conflict between subjective expectations and an uncooperative objective reality. They show a protagonist wrestling with antagonizing forces, not a rosy picture of results meeting expectations—which no one ends up believing.

Consider the CEO of a biotech start-up who has discovered a chemical to prevent heart attacks. He could make a pitch to investors by offering up market projections, the business plan, and upbeat, hypothetical scenarios. Or he could captivate them by telling the story of his father, who died of a heart attack, and the CEO's subsequent struggle against various antagonists—nature, the FDA, potential rivals—to bring to market the effective, low-cost test that might have prevented his father's death.

Good storytellers are not necessarily good leaders, but they do share certain traits. Both are self-aware, and both are skeptics who realize that all people—and institutions—wear masks. Compelling stories can be found beneath those masks.

The other way to persuade people—and ultimately a much more powerful way—is by uniting an idea with an emotion. The best way to do that is by telling a compelling story. In a story, you not only weave a lot of information into the telling but you also arouse your listener's emotions and energy. Persuading with a story is hard. Any intelligent person can sit down and make lists. It takes rationality but little creativity to design an argument using conventional rhetoric. But it demands vivid insight and storytelling skill to present an idea that packs enough emotional power to be memorable. If you can harness imagination and the principles of a well-told story, then you get people rising to their feet amid thunderous applause instead of yawning and ignoring you.

So, what is a story?

Essentially, a story expresses how and why life changes. It begins with a situation in which life is relatively in balance: You come to work day after day, week after week, and everything's fine. You expect it will go on that way. But then there's an event—in screenwriting, we call it the "inciting incident"—that throws life out of balance. You get a new job, or the boss dies of a heart attack, or a big customer threatens to leave. The story goes on to describe how, in an effort to restore balance, the protagonist's subjective expectations crash into an uncooperative objective reality. A good storyteller describes what it's like to deal with these opposing forces, calling on the protagonist to dig deeper, work with scarce resources, make difficult decisions, take action despite risks, and ultimately discover the truth. All great storytellers since the dawn of time—from the ancient Greeks through Shakespeare and up to the present day—have dealt with this fundamental conflict between subjective expectation and cruel reality.

How would an executive learn to tell stories?

Stories have been implanted in you thousands of times since your mother took you on her knee. You've read good books, seen movies, attended plays. What's more, human beings naturally *want* to work through stories. Cognitive psychologists describe how the human mind, in its attempt to understand and remember, assembles the bits and pieces of experience into a story, beginning with a personal desire, a life objective, and then portraying the struggle against the forces that block that desire. Stories are how we remember; we tend to forget lists and bullet points.

Businesspeople not only have to understand their companies' past, but then they must project the future. And how do you imagine the future? As a story. You create scenarios in your head of possible future events to try to anticipate the life of your company or your own personal life. So, if a businessperson understands that his or her own mind naturally wants to frame experience in a story, the key to moving an audience is not to resist this impulse but to embrace it by telling a good story.

What makes a good story?

You emphatically do not want to tell a beginning-to-end tale describing how results meet expectations. This is boring and banal. Instead, you want to display the struggle between expectation and reality in all its nastiness.

For example, let's imagine the story of a biotech start-up we'll call Chemcorp, whose CEO has to persuade some Wall Street bankers to invest in the company. He could tell them that Chemcorp has discovered a chemical compound that prevents heart attacks and offer up a lot of slides showing them the size of the market, the business plan, the organizational chart, and so on. The bankers would nod politely and stifle yawns while thinking of all the other companies better positioned in Chemcorp's market.

Alternatively, the CEO could turn his pitch into a story, beginning with someone close to him—say, his father—who died of a heart attack. So nature itself is the first antagonist that the CEO-as-protagonist must overcome. The story might unfold like this: In his grief, he realizes that if there had been some chemical indication of heart disease, his father's death could have been prevented. His company discovers a protein that's present in the blood just before heart attacks and develops an easy-to-administer, low-cost test.

But now it faces a new antagonist: the FDA. The approval process is fraught with risks and dangers. The FDA turns down the first application, but new research reveals that the test performs even better than anyone had expected, so the agency approves a second application. Meanwhile, Chemcorp is running out of money, and a key partner drops out and goes off to start his own company. Now Chemcorp is in a fight-to-the-finish patent race.

This accumulation of antagonists creates great suspense. The protagonist has raised the idea in the bankers' heads that the story might not have a happy ending. By now, he has them on the edges of their seats, and he says, "We won the race, we got the patent, we're poised to go public and save a quarter-million lives a year." And the bankers just throw money at him.

Aren't you really talking about exaggeration and manipulation?

No. Although businesspeople are often suspicious of stories for the reasons you suggest, the fact is that statistics are used to tell lies and damn lies, while accounting reports are often BS in a ball gown—witness Enron and WorldCom.

When people ask me to help them turn their presentations into stories, I begin by asking questions. I kind of psychoanalyze their companies, and amazing dramas pour out. But most companies and executives sweep the dirty laundry, the difficulties, the antagonists, and the struggle under the carpet. They prefer to present a rosy— and boring—picture to the world. But as a storyteller, you want to position the problems in the foreground and then show how you've overcome them. When you tell the story of your struggles against real antagonists, your audience sees you as an exciting, dynamic person. And I know that the storytelling method works, because after I consulted with a dozen corporations whose principals told exciting stories to Wall Street, they all got their money.

What's wrong with painting a positive picture?

It doesn't ring true. You can send out a press release talking about increased sales and a bright future, but your audience knows it's never that easy. They know you're not spotless; they know your competitor doesn't wear a black hat. They know you've slanted your statement to make your company look good. Positive, hypothetical pictures and boilerplate press releases actually work against you because they foment distrust among the people you're trying to convince. I suspect that most CEOs do not believe their own spin doctors—and if they don't believe the hype, why should the public?

The great irony of existence is that what makes life worth living does not come from the rosy side. We would all rather be lotus-eaters, but life will not allow it. The energy to live comes from the dark side. It comes from everything that makes us suffer. As we struggle against these negative powers, we're forced to live more deeply, more fully.

So acknowledging this dark side makes you more convincing?

Of course. Because you're more truthful. One of the principles of good storytelling is the understanding that we all live in dread. Fear is when you don't know what's going to happen. Dread is when you know what's going to happen and there's nothing you can do to stop it. Death is the great dread; we all live in an ever shrinking shadow of time, and between now and then all kinds of bad things could happen.

Most of us repress this dread. We get rid of it by inflicting it on other people through sarcasm, cheating, abuse, indifference—cruelties great and small. We all commit those little evils that relieve the pressure and make us feel better. Then we rationalize our bad behavior and convince ourselves we're good people. Institutions do the same thing: They deny the existence of the negative while inflicting their dread on other institutions or their employees.

If you're a realist, you know that this is human nature; in fact, you realize that this behavior is the foundation of all nature. The imperative in nature is to follow the golden rule of survival: Do unto others what they do unto you. In nature, if you offer cooperation and get cooperation back, you get along. But if you offer cooperation and get antagonism back, then you give antagonism in return—in spades.

Ever since human beings sat around the fire in caves, we've told stories to help us deal with the dread of life and the struggle to survive. All great stories illuminate the dark side. I'm not talking about so-called "pure" evil, because there is no such thing. We are all evil and good, and these sides do continual battle. Kenneth Lay says wiping out people's jobs and life savings was unintentional. Hannibal Lecter is witty, charming, and brilliant, and he eats people's livers. Audiences appreciate the truthfulness of a storyteller who acknowledges the dark side of human beings and deals honestly with antagonistic events. The story engenders a positive but realistic energy in the people who hear it.

Does this mean you have to be a pessimist?

It's not a question of whether you're optimistic or pessimistic. It seems to me that the civilized human being is a skeptic—someone who believes nothing at face value. Skepticism is another principle of the storyteller. The skeptic understands the difference between text and subtext and always seeks what's really going on. The skeptic hunts for the truth beneath the surface of life, knowing that the real thoughts and feelings of institutions or individuals are unconscious and unexpressed. The skeptic is always looking behind the mask. Street kids, for example, with their tattoos, piercings, chains, and leather, wear amazing masks, but the skeptic knows the mask is only a persona. Inside anyone working that hard to look fierce is a marshmallow. Genuinely hard people make no effort.

So, a story that embraces darkness produces a positive energy in listeners?

Absolutely. We follow people in whom we believe. The best leaders I've dealt with—producers and directors—have come to terms with dark reality. Instead of communicating via spin doctors, they lead their actors and crews through the antagonism of a world in which the odds of getting the film made, distributed, and sold to millions of moviegoers are a thousand to one. They appreciate that the people who work for them love the work and live for the small triumphs that contribute to the final triumph.

CEOs, likewise, have to sit at the head of the table or in front of the microphone and navigate their companies through the storms of bad economies and tough competition. If you look your audience in the eye, lay out your really scary challenges, and say, "We'll be lucky as hell if we get through this, but here's what I think we should do," they will listen to you.

To get people behind you, you can tell a truthful story. The story of General Electric is wonderful and has nothing to do with Jack Welch's cult of celebrity. If you have a grand view of life, you can see it on all its complex levels and celebrate it in a story. A great CEO is someone who has come to terms with his or her own mortality and, as a result, has compassion for others. This compassion is expressed in stories.

Take the love of work, for example. Years ago, when I was in graduate school, I worked as an insurance fraud investigator. The claimant in one case was an immigrant who'd suffered a terrible head injury on a carmaker's assembly line. He'd been the fastest window assembler on the line and took great pride in his work. When I spoke to him, he was waiting to have a titanium plate inserted into his head.

The man had been grievously injured, but the company thought he was a fraud. In spite of that, he remained incredibly dedicated. All he wanted was to get back to work. He knew the value of work, no matter how repetitive. He took pride in it and even in the company that had falsely accused him. How wonderful it would have been for the CEO of that car company to tell the tale of how his managers recognized the falseness of their accusation and then rewarded the employee for his dedication. The company, in turn, would have been rewarded with redoubled effort from all the employees who heard that story.

How do storytellers discover and unearth the stories that want to be told?

The storyteller discovers a story by asking certain key questions. First, what does my protagonist want in order to restore balance in his or her life? Desire is the blood of a story. Desire is not a shopping list but a core need that, if satisfied, would stop the story in its tracks. Next, what is keeping my protagonist from achieving his or her desire? Forces within? Doubt? Fear? Confusion? Personal conflicts with friends, family, lovers? Social conflicts arising in the various institutions in society? Physical conflicts? The forces of Mother Nature? Lethal diseases in the air? Not enough time to get things done? The damned automobile that won't start? Antagonists come from people, society, time, space, and every object in it, or any combination of these forces at once. Then, how would my protagonist decide to act in order to achieve his or her desire in the face of these antagonistic forces? It's in the answer to that question that storytellers discover the truth of their characters, because the heart of a human being is revealed in the choices he or she makes under pressure. Finally, the storyteller leans back from the design of events he or she has created and asks, "Do I believe this? Is it neither an exaggeration nor a soft-soaping of the struggle? Is this an honest telling, though heaven may fall?"

Does being a good storyteller make you a good leader?

Not necessarily, but if you understand the principles of storytelling, you probably have a good understanding of yourself and of human nature, and that tilts the odds in your favor. I can teach the formal principles of stories, but not to a person who hasn't really lived. The art of storytelling takes intelligence, but it also demands a life experience that I've noted in gifted film directors: the pain of childhood. Childhood trauma forces you into a kind of mild schizophrenia that makes you see life simultaneously in two ways: First, it's direct, real-time experience, but at the same moment, your brain records it as material—material out of which you will create business ideas, science, or art. Like a double-edged knife, the creative mind cuts to the truth of self and the humanity of others.

Self-knowledge is the root of all great storytelling. A storyteller creates all characters from the self by asking the question, "If I were this character in these circumstances, what would I do?" The more you understand your own humanity, the more you can appreciate the humanity of others in all their good-versus-evil struggles. I would argue that the great leaders Jim Collins describes are people with enormous self-knowledge. They have self-insight and self-respect balanced by skepticism. Great storytellers—and, I suspect, great leaders—are skeptics who understand their own masks as well as the masks of life, and this understanding makes them humble. They see the humanity in others and deal with them in a compassionate yet realistic way. That duality makes for a wonderful leader.

Originally published in June 2003. Reprint R0306B

Connect, Then Lead

by Amy J.C. Cuddy, Matthew Kohut,
and John Neffinger

IS IT BETTER TO BE LOVED OR FEARED? Niccolò Machiavelli pondered that timeless conundrum 500 years ago and hedged his bets. "It may be answered that one should wish to be both," he acknowledged, "but because it is difficult to unite them in one person, it is much safer to be feared than loved."

Now behavioral science is weighing in with research showing that Machiavelli had it partly right: When we judge others—especially our leaders—we look first at two characteristics: how lovable they are (their warmth, communion, or trustworthiness) and how fearsome they are (their strength, agency, or competence). Although there is some disagreement about the proper labels for the traits, researchers agree that they are the two primary dimensions of social judgment.

Why are these traits so important? Because they answer two critical questions: "What are this person's intentions toward me?" and "Is he or she capable of acting on those intentions?" Together, these assessments underlie our emotional and behavioral reactions to other people, groups, and even brands and companies. Research by one of us, Amy Cuddy, and colleagues Susan Fiske, of Princeton, and Peter Glick, of Lawrence University, shows that people judged to be competent but lacking in warmth often elicit envy in others, an emotion involving both respect and resentment that cuts both ways. When we respect someone, we want to cooperate or affiliate ourselves with him or her, but resentment can make that person vulnerable to harsh reprisal (think of disgraced Tyco CEO Dennis Kozlowski, whose extravagance made him an unsympathetic public figure). On the other hand, people judged as warm but incompetent tend to elicit pity, which also involves a mix of emotions: Compassion moves us to help those we pity, but our lack of respect leads us ultimately to neglect them (think of workers who become marginalized as they near retirement or of an employee with outmoded skills in a rapidly evolving industry).

To be sure, we notice plenty of other traits in people, but they're nowhere near as influential as warmth and strength. Indeed, insights from the field of psychology show that these two dimensions account for more than 90% of the variance in our positive or negative impressions we form of the people around us.

So which is better, being lovable or being strong? Most leaders today tend to emphasize their strength, competence, and credentials in the workplace, but that is exactly the wrong approach. Leaders who project strength before establishing trust run the risk of eliciting fear, and along with it a host of dysfunctional behaviors. Fear can undermine cognitive potential, creativity, and problem solving, and cause employees to get stuck and even disengage. It's a "hot" emotion, with long-lasting effects. It burns into our memory in a way that cooler emotions don't. Research by Jack Zenger and Joseph Folkman drives this point home: In a study of 51,836 leaders, only 27 of them were rated in the bottom quartile in terms of likability and in the top quartile in terms of overall leadership effectiveness—in other words, the chances that a manager who is strongly disliked will be considered a good leader are only about one in 2,000.

A growing body of research suggests that the way to influence—and to lead—is to begin with warmth. Warmth is the conduit of influence: It facilitates trust and the communication and absorption of ideas. Even a few small nonverbal signals—a nod, a smile, an open gesture—can show people that you're pleased to be in their company and attentive to their concerns. Prioritizing warmth helps you connect immediately with those around you, demonstrating that you hear them, understand them, and can be trusted by them.

Idea in Brief

The Problem

Typically, leaders emphasize their strength or competence in the workplace, which can alienate colleagues and direct reports.

The Argument

Decades of sociology and psychology research show that by first focusing on displaying warmth—and then blending in demonstrations

of competence—leaders will find a clearer path to influence.

The Lessons

This is difficult to do but not impossible, depending on your chemical and dispositional makeup. The authors offer specific guidelines on how to project warmth and strength in various situations.

When Strength Comes First

Most of us work hard to demonstrate our competence. We want to see ourselves as strong—and want others to see us the same way. We focus on warding off challenges to our strength and providing abundant evidence of competence. We feel compelled to demonstrate that we're up to the job, by striving to present the most innovative ideas in meetings, being the first to tackle a challenge, and working the longest hours. We're sure of our own intentions and thus don't feel the need to prove that we're trustworthy—despite the fact that evidence of trustworthiness is the first thing we look for in others.

Organizational psychologists Andrea Abele, of the University of Erlangen-Nuremberg, and Bogdan Wojciszke, of the University of Gdańsk, have documented this phenomenon across a variety of settings. In one experiment, when asked to choose between training programs focusing on competence-related skills (such as time management) and warmth-related ones (providing social support, for instance), most participants opted for competence-based training for themselves but soft-skills training for others. In another experiment, in which participants were asked to describe an event that shaped their self-image, most told stories about themselves that emphasized their own competence and self-determination ("I passed my pilot's license test on the first try"), whereas when they described a similar event for someone else, they focused on that person's warmth and generosity ("My friend tutored his neighbor's child in math and refused to accept any payment").

But putting competence first undermines leadership: Without a foundation of trust, people in the organization may comply outwardly with a leader's wishes, but they're much less likely to conform privately—to adopt the values, culture, and mission of the organization in a sincere, lasting way. Workplaces lacking in trust often have a culture of "every employee for himself," in which people feel that they must be vigilant about protecting their interests. Employees can become reluctant to help others because they're unsure of whether their efforts will be reciprocated or recognized. The result: Shared organizational resources fall victim to the tragedy of the commons.

When Warmth Comes First

Although most of us strive to demonstrate our strength, warmth contributes significantly more to others' evaluations of us—and it's judged before competence. Princeton social psychologist Alex Todorov and colleagues study the cognitive and neural mechanisms that drive our "spontaneous trait inferences"—the snap judgments we make when briefly looking at faces. Their research shows that when making those judgments, people consistently pick up on warmth faster than on competence. This preference for warmth holds true in other areas as well. In a study led by Oscar Ybarra, of the University of Michigan, participants playing a word game identified warmth-related words (such as "friendly") significantly faster than competence-related ones (such as "skillful").

Behavioral economists, for their part, have shown that judgments of trustworthiness generally lead to significantly higher economic gains. For example, Mascha van 't Wout, of Brown University, and Alan Sanfey, of the University of Arizona, asked subjects to determine how an endowment should be allocated. Players invested more

How Will People React to Your Style?

RESEARCH BY AMY CUDDY, Susan Fiske, and Peter Glick suggests that the way others perceive your levels of warmth and competence determines the emotions you'll elicit and your ability to influence a situation. For example, if you're highly competent but show only moderate warmth, you'll get people to go along with you, but you won't earn their true engagement and support. And if you show no warmth, beware of those who may try to derail your efforts—and maybe your career.

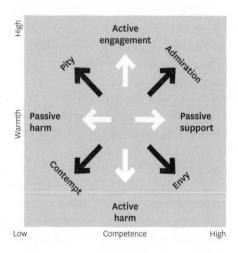

money, with no guarantee of return, in partners whom they perceived to be more trustworthy on the basis of a glance at their faces.

In management settings, trust increases information sharing, openness, fluidity, and cooperation. If coworkers can be trusted to do the right thing and live up to their commitments, planning, coordination, and execution are much easier. Trust also facilitates the exchange and acceptance of ideas—it allows people to hear others' message—and boosts the quantity and quality of the ideas that are produced within an organization. Most important, trust provides the opportunity to change people's attitudes and beliefs, not just their outward behavior. That's the sweet spot when it comes to influence and the ability to get people to fully accept your message.

The Happy Warrior

The best way to gain influence is to combine warmth and strength—as difficult as Machiavelli says that may be to do. The traits can actually be mutually reinforcing: Feeling a sense of personal strength helps us to be more open, less threatened, and less threatening in stressful situations. When we feel confident and calm, we project authenticity and warmth.

Understanding a little bit about our chemical makeup can shed some light on how this works. The neuropeptides oxytocin and arginine vasopressin, for instance, have been linked to our ability to form human attachments, to feel and express warmth, and to behave altruistically. Recent research also suggests that across the animal kingdom, feelings of strength and power have close ties to two hormones: testosterone (associated with assertiveness, reduced fear, and willingness to compete and take risks) and cortisol (associated with stress and stress reactivity).

One study, by Jennifer Lerner, Gary Sherman, Amy Cuddy, and colleagues, brought hundreds of people participating in Harvard executive-education programs into the lab and compared their levels of cortisol with the average levels of the general population. The leaders reported less stress and anxiety than did the general population, and their physiology backed that up: Their cortisol levels were significantly lower. Moreover, the higher their rank and the more subordinates they managed, the lower their cortisol level. Why? Most likely because the leaders had a heightened sense of control—a psychological factor known to have a powerful stress-buffering effect. According to research by Pranjal Mehta, of the University of Oregon, and Robert Josephs, of the University of Texas, the most effective leaders, regardless of gender, have a unique physiological profile, with relatively high testosterone and relatively low cortisol.

Such leaders face troubles without being troubled. Their behavior is not relaxed, but they are relaxed emotionally. They're often viewed as "happy warriors," and the effect of their demeanor on those around them is compelling. Happy warriors reassure us that whatever challenges we may face, things will work out in the end. Ann Richards, the former governor of Texas, played the happy warrior by pairing her

Why Warmth Trumps Strength

THE PRIMACY OF WARMTH manifests in many interrelated ways that powerfully underscore the importance of connecting with people before trying to lead them.

The Need to Affiliate

People have a need to be included, to feel a sense of belonging. In fact, some psychologists would argue that the drive to affiliate ranks among our primary needs as humans. Experiments by neuroscientist Naomi Eisenberger and colleagues suggest that the need is so strong that when we are ostracized—even by virtual strangers—we experience pain that is akin to strong physical pain.

"Us" Versus "Them"

In recent decades, few areas have received as much attention from social psychology researchers as group dynamics—and for good reason: The preference for the groups to which one belongs is so strong that even under extreme conditions—such as knowing that membership in a group was randomly assigned and that the groups themselves are arbitrary—people consistently prefer fellow group members to nonmembers. As a leader, you must make sure you're a part of the key groups in your organization. In fact, you want to be the aspirational member of the group, the chosen representative of the group. As soon as you become one of "them"—the management, the leadership—you begin to lose people.

The Desire to Be Understood

People deeply desire to be heard and seen. Sadly, as important as perspective-taking is to good leadership, being in a position of power decreases people's understanding of others' points of view. When we have power over others, our ability to see them as individuals diminishes. So leaders need to consciously and consistently make the effort to imagine walking in the shoes of the people they are leading.

assertiveness and authority with a big smile and a quick wit that made it clear she did not let the rough-and-tumble of politics get her down.

During crises, these are the people who are able to keep that influence conduit open and may even expand it. Most people hate uncertainty, but they tolerate it much better when they can look to a leader who they believe has their back and is calm, clearheaded, and courageous. These are the people we trust. These are the people we listen to.

There are physical exercises that can help to summon self-confidence—and even alter your body's chemistry to be more like that of a happy warrior. Dana Carney, Amy Cuddy, and Andy Yap suggest that people adopt "power poses" associated with dominance and strength across the animal kingdom. These postures are open, expansive, and space-occupying (imagine Wonder Woman and Superman standing tall with their hands on their hips and feet spread apart). By adopting these postures for just two minutes prior to social encounters, their research shows, participants significantly increased their testosterone and decreased their cortisol levels.

Bear in mind that the signals we send can be ambiguous—we can see someone's reaction to our presence, but we may not be sure exactly what the person is reacting to. We may feel a leader's warmth but remain unsure whether it is directed at us; we sense her strength but need reassurance that it is squarely aimed at the shared challenge we face. And, as we noted earlier, judgments are often made quickly, on the basis of nonverbal cues. Especially when facing a high-pressure situation, it is useful for leaders to go through a brief warm-up routine beforehand to get in the right state of mind, practicing and adopting an attitude that will help them project positive nonverbal signals. We refer to this approach as "inside-out," in contrast to the "outside-in" strategy of trying to consciously execute specific nonverbal behaviors in the moment. Think of the difference between method acting and classical acting: In method acting, the actor experiences the emotions of the character and naturally produces an authentic performance, whereas in classical acting, actors learn to exercise precise control of their nonverbal signals. Generally speaking, an inside-out approach is more effective.

There are many tactics for projecting warmth and competence, and these can be dialed up or down as needed. Two of us, John Neffinger and Matt Kohut, work with leaders from many walks of life in mastering both nonverbal and verbal cues. Let's look now at some best practices.

How to Project Warmth

Efforts to appear warm and trustworthy by consciously controlling your nonverbal signals can backfire: All too often, you'll come off as wooden and inauthentic instead. Here are ways to avoid that trap.

Find the right level

When people want to project warmth, they sometimes amp up the enthusiasm in their voice, increasing their volume and dynamic range to convey delight. That can be effective in the right setting, but if those around you have done nothing in particular to earn your adulation, they'll assume either that you're faking it or that you fawn over everyone indiscriminately.

A better way to create vocal warmth is to speak with lower pitch and volume, as you would if you were comforting a friend. Aim for a tone that suggests that you're leveling with people—that you're sharing the straight scoop, with no pretense or emotional adornment. In doing so, you signal that you trust those you're talking with to handle things the right way. You might even occasionally share a personal story—one that feels private but not inappropriate—in a confiding tone of voice to demonstrate that you're being forthcoming and open. Suppose, for instance, that you want to establish a bond with new employees you're meeting for the first time. You might offer something personal right off the bat, such as recalling how you felt at a similar point in your career. That's often enough to set a congenial tone.

Validate feelings

Before people decide what they think of your message, they decide what they think of *you*. If you show your employees that you hold roughly the same worldview they do, you demonstrate not only empathy but, in their eyes, common sense—the ultimate qualification for being listened to. So if you want colleagues to listen and agree with you, first agree with them.

Imagine, for instance, that your company is undergoing a major reorganization and your group is feeling deep anxiety over what the change could mean—for quality, innovation, job security. Acknowledge people's fear and concerns when you speak to them, whether in formal meetings or during watercooler chats. Look them in the eye and say, "I know everybody's feeling a lot of uncertainty right now, and it's unsettling." People will respect you for addressing the elephant in the room, and will be more open to hearing what you have to say.

Smile—and mean it

When we smile sincerely, the warmth becomes self-reinforcing: Feeling happy makes us smile, and smiling makes us happy. This facial feedback is also contagious. We tend to mirror one another's nonverbal expressions and emotions, so when we see someone beaming and emanating genuine warmth, we can't resist smiling ourselves.

Warmth is not easy to fake, of course, and a polite smile fools no one. To project warmth, you have to genuinely feel it. A natural smile, for instance, involves not only the muscles around the mouth but also those around the eyes—the crow's feet.

So how do you produce a natural smile? Find some reason to feel happy wherever you may be, even if you have to resort to laughing at your predicament. Introverts in social settings can single out one person to focus on. This can help you channel the sense of comfort you feel with close friends or family.

For example, KNP worked with a manager who was having trouble connecting with her employees. Having come up through the ranks as a highly analytic engineer, she projected competence and determination, but not much warmth. We noticed, however, that when she talked about where she grew up and what she learned about life from the tight-knit community in her neighborhood, her demeanor relaxed and she smiled broadly. By including a brief anecdote about her upbringing when she kicked off a meeting or made a presentation, she was able to show her colleagues a warm and relatable side of herself.

One thing to avoid: smiling with your eyebrows raised at anyone over the age of five. This suggests that you are overly eager to please

Are You Projecting Warmth?

HOW YOU PRESENT YOURSELF in workplace settings matters a great deal to how you're perceived by others. Even if you're not feeling particularly warm, practicing these approaches and using them in formal and informal situations can help clear your path to influence.

Warm

When standing, balance your weight primarily on one hip to avoid appearing rigid or tense.

Tilt your head slightly and keep your hands open and welcoming.

Cold

Avoid standing with your chin pointed down.

Don't pivot your body away from the person you're engaging with.

Avoid closed-hand positions and cutting motions.

Lean inward in a nonaggressive manner to signal interest and engagement.

Place your hands comfortably on your knees or rest them on the table.

Aim for body language that feels professional but relaxed.

Try not to angle your body away from the person you're engaging.

Crossing your arms indicates coldness and a lack of receptivity.

Avoid sitting "at attention" or in an aggressive posture.

and be liked. It also signals anxiety, which, like warmth, is contagious. It will cost you much more in strength than you will gain in warmth.

How to Project Strength

Strength or competence can be established by virtue of the position you hold, your reputation, and your actual performance. But your presence, or demeanor, always counts, too. The way you carry yourself doesn't establish your skill level, of course, but it is taken as strong evidence of your attitude—how serious you are and how determined to tackle a challenge—and that is an important component of overall strength. The trick is to cultivate a demeanor of strength without seeming menacing.

Feel in command

Warmth may be harder to fake, but confidence is harder to talk yourself into. Feeling like an impostor—that you don't belong in the position you're in and are going to be "found out"—is very common. But self-doubt completely undermines your ability to project confidence, enthusiasm, and passion, the qualities that make up presence. In fact, if you see yourself as an impostor, others will, too. Feeling in command and confident is about connecting with yourself. And when we are connected with ourselves, it is much easier to connect with others.

Holding your body in certain ways, as we discussed above, can help. Although we refer to these postures as power poses, they don't increase your dominance over others. They're about personal power—your agency and ability to self-regulate. Recent research led by Dacher Keltner, of the University of California, Berkeley, shows that feeling powerful in this way allows you to shed the fears and inhibitions that can prevent you from bringing your fullest, most authentic and enthusiastic self to a high-stakes professional situation, such as a pitch to investors or a speech to an influential audience.

Stand up straight

It is hard to overstate the importance of good posture in projecting authority and an intention to be taken seriously. As Maya Angelou wrote, "Stand up straight and realize who you are, that you tower over your circumstances." Good posture does not mean the exaggerated chest-out pose known in the military as standing at attention, or raising one's chin up high. It just means reaching your full height, using your muscles to straighten the S-curve in your spine rather than slouching. It sounds trivial, but maximizing the physical space your body takes up makes a substantial difference in how your audience reacts to you, regardless of your height.

Get ahold of yourself

When you move, move deliberately and precisely to a specific spot rather than casting your limbs about loose-jointedly. And when you are finished moving, be still. Twitching, fidgeting, or other visual static sends the signal that you're not in control. Stillness demonstrates calm. Combine that with good posture, and you'll achieve what's known as poise, which telegraphs equilibrium and stability, important aspects of credible leadership presence.

Standing tall is an especially good way to project strength because it doesn't interfere with warmth in the way that other signals of strength—cutting gestures, a furrowed brow, an elevated chin—often do. People who instruct their children to stand up straight and smile are on to something: This simple combination is perhaps the best way to project strength and warmth simultaneously.

If you want to effectively lead others, you have to get the warmth-competence dynamic right. Projecting both traits at once is difficult, but the two can be mutually reinforcing—and the rewards substantial. Earning the trust and appreciation of those around you feels good. Feeling in command of a situation does, too. Doing both lets you influence people more effectively.

The strategies we suggest may seem awkward at first, but they will soon create a positive feedback loop. Being calm and confident creates space to be warm, open, and appreciative, to choose to act in ways that reflect and express your values and priorities. Once you establish your warmth, your strength is received as a welcome reassurance. Your leadership becomes not a threat but a gift.

Originally published in July 2013. Reprint R1307C

The Necessary Art of Persuasion

by Jay A. Conger

IF THERE EVER WAS A time for businesspeople to learn the fine art of persuasion, it is now. Gone are the command-and-control days of executives managing by decree. Today businesses are run largely by cross-functional teams of peers and populated by baby boomers and their Generation X offspring, who show little tolerance for unquestioned authority. Electronic communication and globalization have further eroded the traditional hierarchy, as ideas and people flow more freely than ever around organizations and as decisions get made closer to the markets. These fundamental changes, more than a decade in the making but now firmly part of the economic landscape, essentially come down to this: work today gets done in an environment where people don't just ask What should I do? but Why should I do it?

To answer this why question effectively is to persuade. Yet many businesspeople misunderstand persuasion, and more still underutilize it. The reason? Persuasion is widely perceived as a skill reserved for selling products and closing deals. It is also commonly seen as just another form of manipulation—devious and to be avoided. Certainly, persuasion can be used in selling and deal-clinching situations, and it can be misused to manipulate people. But exercised constructively and to its full potential, persuasion supersedes sales and is quite the opposite of deception. Effective persuasion becomes a negotiating and learning process through which a persuader leads colleagues to a problem's shared solution. Persuasion does indeed involve moving people to a position they don't currently hold, but not by begging or cajoling. Instead, it involves careful preparation, the proper framing of arguments, the presentation of vivid supporting evidence, and the effort to find the correct emotional match with your audience.

Effective persuasion is a difficult and time-consuming proposition, but it may also be more powerful than the command-and-control managerial model it succeeds. As AlliedSignal's CEO Lawrence Bossidy said recently, "The day when you could yell and scream and beat people into good performance is over. Today you have to appeal to them by helping them see how they can get from here to there, by establishing some credibility, and by giving them some reason and help to get there. Do all those things, and they'll knock down doors." In essence, he is describing persuasion—now more than ever, the language of business leadership.

Think for a moment of your definition of persuasion. If you are like most businesspeople I have encountered, you see persuasion as a relatively straightforward process. First, you strongly state your position. Second, you outline the supporting arguments, followed by a highly assertive, data-based exposition. Finally, you enter the deal-making stage and work toward a "close." In other words, you use logic, persistence, and personal enthusiasm to get others to buy a good idea. The reality is that following this process is one sure-fire way to fail at persuasion. (See the sidebar "Four Ways Not to Persuade.")

What, then, constitutes effective persuasion? If persuasion is a learning and negotiating process, then in the most general terms it involves phases of discovery, preparation, and dialogue. Getting ready to persuade colleagues can take weeks or months of planning as you learn about your audience and the position you intend to argue. Before they even start to talk, effective persuaders have considered their positions from every angle. What investments in time and money will my position require from others? Is my supporting evidence weak in any way? Are there alternative positions I need to examine?

Idea in Brief

This article defines and explains the four essential elements of persuasion. Business today is largely run by teams and populated by authority-averse baby boomers and Generation Xers. That makes persuasion more important than ever as a managerial tool. But contrary to popular belief, author Jay Conger (director of the University of Southern California's Marshall Business School's Leadership Institute) asserts, persuasion is not the same as selling an idea or convincing opponents to see things your way. It is instead a process of learning from others and negotiating a shared solution. To that end, persuasion consists of these essential elements: establishing credibility, framing to find common ground, providing vivid evidence, and connecting emotionally. Credibility grows, the author says, out of two sources: expertise and relationships. The former is a function of product or process knowledge and the latter a history of listening to and working in the best interest of others. But even if a persuader's credibility is high, his position must make sense—even more, it must appeal—to the audience. Therefore, a persuader must frame his position to illuminate its benefits to everyone who will feel its impact. Persuasion then becomes a matter of presenting evidence—but not just ordinary charts and spreadsheets. The author says the most effective persuaders use vivid—even over-the-top—stories, metaphors, and examples to make their positions come alive. Finally, good persuaders have the ability to accurately sense and respond to their audience's emotional state. Sometimes, that means they have to suppress their own emotions; at other times, they must intensify them. Persuasion can be a force for enormous good in an organization, but people must understand it for what it is: an often painstaking process that requires insight, planning, and compromise.

Dialogue happens before and during the persuasion process. Before the process begins, effective persuaders use dialogue to learn more about their audience's opinions, concerns, and perspectives. During the process, dialogue continues to be a form of learning, but it is also the beginning of the negotiation stage. You invite people to discuss, even debate, the merits of your position, and then to offer honest feedback and suggest alternative solutions. That may sound like a slow way to achieve your goal, but effective persuasion is about testing and revising ideas in concert with your colleagues'

Idea in Practice

The process of persuasion has four steps:

1. **Establish credibility.** Your credibility grows out of two sources: **expertise** and **relationships.** If you have a history of well-informed, sound judgment, your colleagues will trust your expertise. If you've demonstrated that you can work in the best interest of others, your colleagues will have confidence in your relationships.

If you are weak on the expertise side, bolster your position by

- learning more through formal and informal education—for example, conversations with in-house experts

- hiring recognized outside experts

- launching pilot projects

To fill in the relationship gap, try

- meeting one-on-one with key people

- involving like-minded co-workers who have good support with your audience

Example: Two developers at Microsoft envisioned a controversial new software product, but both were technology novices. By working closely with technical experts and market testing a prototype, they persuaded management that the new product was ideally suited to the average computer user. It sold half a million units.

2. **Frame goals on common ground.** Tangibly describe the benefits of your position. The fastest way to get a child to the grocery store is to point out the lollipops by the cash register. That is not

concerns and needs. In fact, the best persuaders not only listen to others but also incorporate their perspectives into a shared solution.

Persuasion, in other words, often involves—indeed, demands— compromise. Perhaps that is why the most effective persuaders seem to share a common trait: they are open-minded, never dogmatic. They enter the persuasion process prepared to adjust their viewpoints and incorporate others' ideas. That approach to persuasion is, interestingly, highly persuasive in itself. When colleagues see that a persuader is eager to hear their views and willing to make changes in response to their needs and concerns, they respond very positively. They trust the persuader more and listen more atten-

deception—it's persuasion. When no shared advantages are apparent, adjust your position.

Example: An ad agency executive persuaded skeptical fast-food franchisees to support headquarters' new price discounts. She cited reliable research showing how the pricing scheme improved franchisees' profits. They supported the new plan unanimously.

3. **Vividly reinforce your position.** Ordinary evidence won't do. Make numerical data more compelling with examples, stories, and metaphors that have an emotional impact.

Example: The founder of Mary Kay Cosmetics made a speech comparing sales people's weekly meetings to gatherings among Christians resisting Roman rule. This drove home the importance of a mutually supportive sales force and imbued the work with a sense of heroic mission.

4. **Connect emotionally.** Adjust your own emotional tone to match each audience's ability to receive your message. Learn how your colleagues have interpreted past events in the organization and sense how they will probably interpret your proposal. Test key individuals' possible reactions.

Example: A Chrysler team leader raised the morale of employees demoralized by foreign competition and persuaded management to bring a new car design in-house. He showed both audiences slides of his hometown, which had been devastated by foreign mining competition. His patriotic appeal reinvigorated his team, and the chairman approved the plan.

tively. They don't fear being bowled over or manipulated. They see the persuader as flexible and are thus more willing to make sacrifices themselves. Because that is such a powerful dynamic, good persuaders often enter the persuasion process with judicious compromises already prepared.

Four Essential Steps

Effective persuasion involves four distinct and essential steps. First, effective persuaders establish credibility. Second, they frame their goals in a way that identifies common ground with those they

Four Ways Not to Persuade

IN MY WORK WITH MANAGERS as a researcher and as a consultant, I have had the unfortunate opportunity to see executives fail miserably at persuasion. Here are the four most common mistakes people make:

1. **They attempt to make their case with an up-front, hard sell.** I call this the John Wayne approach. Managers strongly state their position at the outset, and then through a process of persistence, logic, and exuberance, they try to push the idea to a close. In reality, setting out a strong position at the start of a persuasion effort gives potential opponents something to grab onto—and fight against. It's far better to present your position with the finesse and reserve of a lion tamer, who engages his "partner" by showing him the legs of a chair. In other words, effective persuaders don't begin the process by giving their colleagues a clear target in which to set their jaws.

2. **They resist compromise.** Too many managers see compromise as surrender, but it is essential to constructive persuasion. Before people buy into a proposal, they want to see that the persuader is flexible enough to respond to their concerns. Compromises can often lead to better, more sustainable shared solutions.

   By not compromising, ineffective persuaders unconsciously send the message that they think persuasion is a one-way street. But persuasion

intend to persuade. Third, they reinforce their positions using vivid language and compelling evidence. And fourth, they connect emotionally with their audience. As one of the most effective executives in our research commented, "The most valuable lesson I've learned about persuasion over the years is that there's just as much strategy in how you present your position as in the position itself. In fact, I'd say the strategy of presentation is the more critical."

Establish credibility

The first hurdle persuaders must overcome is their own credibility. A persuader can't advocate a new or contrarian position without having people wonder, "Can we trust this individual's perspectives and opinions?" Such a reaction is understandable. After all, allowing oneself to be persuaded is risky, because any new initiative demands

is a process of give-and-take. Kathleen Reardon, a professor of organizational behavior at the University of Southern California, points out that a persuader rarely changes another person's behavior or viewpoint without altering his or her own in the process. To persuade meaningfully, we must not only listen to others but also incorporate their perspectives into our own.

3. **They think the secret of persuasion lies in presenting great arguments.** In persuading people to change their minds, great arguments matter. No doubt about it. But arguments, per se, are only one part of the equation. Other factors matter just as much, such as the persuader's credibility and his or her ability to create a proper, mutually beneficial frame for a position, connect on the right emotional level with an audience, and communicate through vivid language that makes arguments come alive.

4. **They assume persuasion is a one-shot effort.** Persuasion is a process, not an event. Rarely, if ever, is it possible to arrive at a shared solution on the first try. More often than not, persuasion involves listening to people, testing a position, developing a new position that reflects input from the group, more testing, incorporating compromises, and then trying again. If this sounds like a slow and difficult process, that's because it is. But the results are worth the effort.

a commitment of time and resources. Yet even though persuaders must have high credibility, our research strongly suggests that most managers overestimate their own credibility—considerably.

In the workplace, credibility grows out of two sources: expertise and relationships. People are considered to have high levels of expertise if they have a history of sound judgment or have proven themselves knowledgeable and well informed about their proposals. For example, in proposing a new product idea, an effective persuader would need to be perceived as possessing a thorough understanding of the product—its specifications, target markets, customers, and competing products. A history of prior successes would further strengthen the persuader's perceived expertise. One extremely successful executive in our research had a track record of 14 years of devising highly effective advertising campaigns. Not surprisingly, he had an easy time winning colleagues over to his position. Another manager had a track record of seven successful new-product launches in a period of five years. He, too, had an advantage when it came to persuading his colleagues to support his next new idea.

On the relationship side, people with high credibility have demonstrated—again, usually over time—that they can be trusted to listen and to work in the best interests of others. They have also consistently shown strong emotional character and integrity; that is, they are not known for mood extremes or inconsistent performance. Indeed, people who are known to be honest, steady, and reliable have an edge when going into any persuasion situation. Because their relationships are robust, they are more apt to be given the benefit of the doubt. One effective persuader in our research was considered by colleagues to be remarkably trustworthy and fair; many people confided in her. In addition, she generously shared credit for good ideas and provided staff with exposure to the company's senior executives. This woman had built strong relationships, which meant her staff and peers were always willing to consider seriously what she proposed.

If expertise and relationships determine credibility, it is crucial that you undertake an honest assessment of where you stand on both criteria before beginning to persuade. To do so, first step back and ask yourself the following questions related to expertise: How will others perceive my knowledge about the strategy, product, or change I am proposing? Do I have a track record in this area that others know about and respect? Then, to assess the strength of your relationship credibility, ask yourself, Do those I am hoping to persuade see me as helpful, trustworthy, and supportive? Will they see me as someone in sync with them—emotionally, intellectually, and politically—on issues like this one? Finally, it is important to note that it is not enough to get your own read on these matters. You must also test your answers with colleagues you trust to give you a reality check. Only then will you have a complete picture of your credibility.

In most cases, that exercise helps people discover that they have some measure of weakness, either on the expertise or on the relationship side of credibility. The challenge then becomes to fill in such gaps.

In general, if your area of weakness is on the expertise side, you have several options:

- First, you can learn more about the complexities of your position through either formal or informal education and through conversations with knowledgeable individuals. You might also get more relevant experience on the job by asking, for instance, to be assigned to a team that would increase your insight into particular markets or products.

- Another alternative is to hire someone to bolster your expertise—for example, an industry consultant or a recognized outside expert, such as a professor. Either one may have the knowledge and experience required to support your position effectively. Similarly, you may tap experts within your organization to advocate your position. Their credibility becomes a substitute for your own.

- You can also utilize other outside sources of information to support your position, such as respected business or trade periodicals, books, independently produced reports, and lectures by experts. In our research, one executive from the clothing industry successfully persuaded his company to reposition an entire product line to a more youthful market after bolstering his credibility with articles by a noted demographer in two highly regarded journals and with two independent market-research studies.

- Finally, you may launch pilot projects to demonstrate on a small scale your expertise and the value of your ideas.

As for filling in the relationship gap:

- You should make a concerted effort to meet one-on-one with all the key people you plan to persuade. This is not the time to outline your position but rather to get a range of perspectives on the issue at hand. If you have the time and resources, you should even offer to help these people with issues that concern them.

- Another option is to involve like-minded coworkers who already have strong relationships with your audience. Again, that is a matter of seeking out substitutes on your own behalf.

For an example of how these strategies can be put to work, consider the case of a chief operating officer of a large retail bank, whom we will call Tom Smith. Although he was new to his job, Smith ardently wanted to persuade the senior management team that the company was in serious trouble. He believed that the bank's overhead was excessive and would jeopardize its position as the industry entered a more competitive era. Most of his colleagues, however, did not see the potential seriousness of the situation. Because the bank had been enormously successful in recent years, they believed changes in the industry posed little danger. In addition to being newly appointed, Smith had another problem: his career had been in financial services, and he was considered an outsider in the world of retail banking. Thus he had few personal connections to draw on as he made his case, nor was he perceived to be particularly knowledgeable about marketplace exigencies.

As a first step in establishing credibility, Smith hired an external consultant with respected credentials in the industry who showed that the bank was indeed poorly positioned to be a low-cost producer. In a series of interactive presentations to the bank's top-level management, the consultant revealed how the company's leading competitors were taking aggressive actions to contain operating costs. He made it clear from these presentations that not cutting costs would soon cause the bank to fall drastically behind the competition. These findings were then distributed in written reports that circulated throughout the bank.

Next, Smith determined that the bank's branch managers were critical to his campaign. The buy-in of those respected and informed individuals would signal to others in the company that his concerns were valid. Moreover, Smith looked to the branch managers because he believed that they could increase his expertise about marketplace trends and also help him test his own assumptions. Thus, for the next three months, he visited every branch in his region of Ontario,

Canada—135 in all. During each visit, he spent time with branch managers, listening to their perceptions of the bank's strengths and weaknesses. He learned firsthand about the competition's initiatives and customer trends, and he solicited ideas for improving the bank's services and minimizing costs. By the time he was through, Smith had a broad perspective on the bank's future that few people even in senior management possessed. And he had built dozens of relationships in the process.

Finally, Smith launched some small but highly visible initiatives to demonstrate his expertise and capabilities. For example, he was concerned about slow growth in the company's mortgage business and the loan officers' resulting slip in morale. So he devised a program in which new mortgage customers would make no payments for the first 90 days. The initiative proved remarkably successful, and in short order Smith appeared to be a far more savvy retail banker than anyone had assumed.

Another example of how to establish credibility comes from Microsoft. In 1990, two product-development managers, Karen Fries and Barry Linnett, came to believe that the market would greatly welcome software that featured a "social interface." They envisioned a package that would employ animated human and animal characters to show users how to go about their computing tasks.

Inside Microsoft, however, employees had immediate concerns about the concept. Software programmers ridiculed the cute characters. Animated characters had been used before only in software for children, making their use in adult environments hard to envision. But Fries and Linnett felt their proposed product had both dynamism and complexity, and they remained convinced that consumers would eagerly buy such programs. They also believed that the home-computer software market—largely untapped at the time and with fewer software standards—would be open to such innovation.

Within the company, Fries had gained quite a bit of relationship credibility. She had started out as a recruiter for the company in 1987 and had worked directly for many of Microsoft's senior executives. They trusted and liked her. In addition, she had been responsible for hiring the company's product and program managers. As a result, she knew all the senior people at Microsoft and had hired many of the people who would be deciding on her product.

Linnett's strength laid in his expertise. In particular, he knew the technology behind an innovative tutorial program called PC Works. In addition, both Fries and Linnett had managed Publisher, a product with a unique help feature called Wizards, which Microsoft's CEO, Bill Gates, had liked. But those factors were sufficient only to get an initial hearing from Microsoft's senior management. To persuade the organization to move forward, the pair would need to improve perceptions of their expertise. It hurt them that this type of social-interface software had no proven track record of success and that they were both novices with such software. Their challenge became one of finding substitutes for their own expertise.

Their first step was a wise one. From within Microsoft, they hired respected technical guru Darrin Massena. With Massena, they developed a set of prototypes to demonstrate that they did indeed understand the software's technology and could make it work. They then tested the prototypes in market research, and users responded enthusiastically. Finally, and most important, they enlisted two Stanford University professors, Clifford Nass and Bryon Reeves, both experts in human-computer interaction. In several meetings with Microsoft senior managers and Gates himself, they presented a rigorously compiled and thorough body of research that demonstrated how and why social-interface software was ideally suited to the average computer user. In addition, Fries and Linnett asserted that considerable jumps in computing power would make more realistic cartoon characters an increasingly malleable technology. Their product, they said, was the leading edge of an incipient software revolution. Convinced, Gates approved a full product-development team, and in January 1995, the product called BOB was launched. BOB went on to sell more than half a million copies, and its concept and technology are being used within Microsoft as a platform for developing several Internet products.

Credibility is the cornerstone of effective persuading; without it, a persuader won't be given the time of day. In the best-case scenario, people enter into a persuasion situation with some measure of expertise and relationship credibility. But it is important to note that credibility along either lines can be built or bought. Indeed, it must be, or the next steps are an exercise in futility.

Frame for common ground

Even if your credibility is high, your position must still appeal strongly to the people you are trying to persuade. After all, few people will jump on board a train that will bring them to ruin or even mild discomfort. Effective persuaders must be adept at describing their positions in terms that illuminate their advantages. As any parent can tell you, the fastest way to get a child to come along willingly on a trip to the grocery store is to point out that there are lollipops by the cash register. That is not deception. It is just a persuasive way of framing the benefits of taking such a journey. In work situations, persuasive framing is obviously more complex, but the underlying principle is the same. It is a process of identifying shared benefits.

Monica Ruffo, an account executive for an advertising agency, offers a good example of persuasive framing. Her client, a fast-food chain, was instituting a promotional campaign in Canada; menu items such as a hamburger, fries, and cola were to be bundled together and sold at a low price. The strategy made sense to corporate headquarters. Its research showed that consumers thought the company's products were higher priced than the competition's, and the company was anxious to overcome this perception. The franchisees, on the other hand, were still experiencing strong sales and were far more concerned about the short-term impact that the new, low prices would have on their profit margins.

A less experienced persuader would have attempted to rationalize headquarters' perspective to the franchisees—to convince them of its validity. But Ruffo framed the change in pricing to demonstrate its benefits to the franchisees themselves. The new value campaign, she explained, would actually improve franchisees' profits. To back up this point, she drew on several sources. A pilot project in Tennessee, for instance, had demonstrated that under the new pricing scheme, the sales of french fries and drinks—the two most profitable items on the menu—had markedly increased. In addition, the company had rolled out medium-sized meal packages in 80% of its U.S. outlets, and franchisees' sales of fries and drinks had jumped 26%. Citing research from a respected business periodical, Ruffo also showed that when customers raised their estimate of the value they receive from a retail establishment by 10%, the establishment's sales rose by 1%. She had estimated that the new meal plan would increase value perceptions by 100%, with the result that franchisee sales could be expected to grow 10%.

Ruffo closed her presentation with a letter written many years before by the company's founder to the organization. It was an emotional letter extolling the values of the company and stressing the importance of the franchisees to the company's success. It also highlighted the importance of the company's position as the low-price leader in the industry. The beliefs and values contained in the letter had long been etched in the minds of Ruffo's audience. Hearing them again only confirmed the company's concern for the franchisees and the importance of their winning formula. They also won Ruffo a standing ovation. That day, the franchisees voted unanimously to support the new meal-pricing plan.

The Ruffo case illustrates why—in choosing appropriate positioning—it is critical first to identify your objective's tangible benefits to the people you are trying to persuade. Sometimes that is easy. Mutual benefits exist. In other situations, however, no shared advantages are readily apparent—or meaningful. In these cases, effective persuaders adjust their positions. They know it is impossible to engage people and gain commitment to ideas or plans without highlighting the advantages to all the parties involved.

At the heart of framing is a solid understanding of your audience. Even before starting to persuade, the best persuaders we have encountered closely study the issues that matter to their colleagues. They use conversations, meetings, and other forms of dialogue to collect essential information. They are good at listening. They test their ideas with trusted confidants, and they ask questions of the people they will later be persuading. Those steps help them think through the arguments, the evidence, and the perspectives they will present. Oftentimes, this process causes them to alter or compromise their own plans before they even start persuading. It is through this thoughtful, inquisitive approach they develop frames that appeal to their audience.

Consider the case of a manager who was in charge of process engineering for a jet engine manufacturer. He had redesigned the work flow for routine turbine maintenance for airline clients in a manner that would dramatically shorten the turnaround time for servicing. Before presenting his ideas to the company's president, he consulted a good friend in the company, the vice president of engineering, who knew the president well. This conversation revealed that the president's prime concern would not be speed or efficiency but profitability. To get the president's buy-in, the vice president explained, the new system would have to improve the company's profitability in the short run by lowering operating expenses.

At first this information had the manager stumped. He had planned to focus on efficiency and had even intended to request additional funding to make the process work. But his conversation with the vice president sparked him to change his position. Indeed, he went so far as to change the work-flow design itself so that it no longer required new investment but rather drove down costs. He then carefully documented the cost savings and profitability gains that his new plan would produce and presented this revised plan to the president. With his initiative positioned anew, the manager persuaded the president and got the project approved.

Provide evidence

With credibility established and a common frame identified, persuasion becomes a matter of presenting evidence. Ordinary evidence, however, won't do. We have found that the most effective persuaders use language in a particular way. They supplement numerical data with examples, stories, metaphors, and analogies to make their positions come alive. That use of language paints a vivid word picture and, in doing so, lends a compelling and tangible quality to the persuader's point of view.

Think about a typical persuasion situation. The persuader is often advocating a goal, strategy, or initiative with an uncertain outcome.

Karen Fries and Barry Linnett, for instance, wanted Microsoft to invest millions of dollars in a software package with chancy technology and unknown market demand. The team could have supported its case solely with market research, financial projections, and the like. But that would have been a mistake, because research shows that most people perceive such reports as not entirely informative. They are too abstract to be completely meaningful or memorable. In essence, the numbers don't make an emotional impact.

By contrast, stories and vivid language do, particularly when they present comparable situations to the one under discussion. A marketing manager trying to persuade senior executives to invest in a new product, for example, might cite examples of similar investments that paid off handsomely. Indeed, we found that people readily draw lessons from such cases. More important, the research shows that listeners absorb information in proportion to its vividness. Thus it is no wonder that Fries and Linnett hit a home run when they presented their case for BOB with the following analogy:

> Imagine you want to cook dinner and you must first go to the supermarket. You have all the flexibility you want—you can cook anything in the world as long as you know how and have the time and desire to do it. When you arrive at the supermarket, you find all these overstuffed aisles with cryptic single-word headings like "sundries" and "ethnic food" and "condiments." These are the menus on typical computer interfaces. The question is whether salt is under condiments or ethnic food or near the potato chip section. There are surrounding racks and wall spaces, much as our software interfaces now have support buttons, tool bars, and lines around the perimeters. Now after you have collected everything, you still need to put it all together in the correct order to make a meal. If you're a good cook, your meal will probably be good. If you're a novice, it probably won't be.
>
> We [at Microsoft] have been selling under the supermarket category for years, and we think there is a big opportunity for restaurants. That's what we are trying to do now with BOB: pushing the next step with software that is more like going to a

restaurant, so the user doesn't spend all of his time searching for the ingredients. We find and put the ingredients together. You sit down, you get comfortable. We bring you a menu. We do the work, you relax. It's an enjoyable experience. No walking around lost trying to find things, no cooking.

Had Fries and Linnett used a literal description of BOB's advantages, few of their highly computer-literate colleagues at Microsoft would have personally related to the menu-searching frustration that BOB was designed to eliminate. The analogy they selected, however, made BOB's purpose both concrete and memorable.

A master persuader, Mary Kay Ash, the founder of Mary Kay Cosmetics, regularly draws on analogies to illustrate and "sell" the business conduct she values. Consider this speech at the company's annual sales convention:

Back in the days of the Roman Empire, the legions of the emperor conquered the known world. There was, however, one band of people that the Romans never conquered. Those people were the followers of the great teacher from Bethlehem. Historians have long since discovered that one of the reasons for the sturdiness of this folk was their habit of meeting together weekly. They shared their difficulties, and they stood side by side. Does this remind you of something? The way we stand side by side and share our knowledge and difficulties with each other in our weekly unit meetings? I have so often observed when a director or unit member is confronted with a personal problem that the unit stands together in helping that sister in distress. What a wonderful circle of friendships we have. Perhaps it's one of the greatest fringe benefits of our company.

Through her vivid analogy, Ash links collective support in the company to a courageous period in Christian history. In doing so, she accomplishes several objectives. First, she drives home her belief that collective support is crucial to the success of the organization. Most Mary Kay salespeople are independent operators who face the daily challenges of direct selling. An emotional support system of fellow salespeople is essential to ensure that self-esteem and confidence remain intact in the face of rejection. Next she suggests by her analogy that solidarity against the odds is the best way to stymie powerful oppressors—to wit, the competition. Finally, Ash's choice of analogy imbues a sense of a heroic mission to the work of her sales force.

You probably don't need to invoke the analogy of the Christian struggle to support your position, but effective persuaders are not afraid of unleashing the immense power of language. In fact, they use it to their utmost advantage.

Connect emotionally

In the business world, we like to think that our colleagues use reason to make their decisions, yet if we scratch below the surface we will always find emotions at play. Good persuaders are aware of the primacy of emotions and are responsive to them in two important ways. First, they show their own emotional commitment to the position they are advocating. Such expression is a delicate matter. If you act too emotional, people may doubt your clearheadedness. But you must also show that your commitment to a goal is not just in your mind but in your heart and gut as well. Without this demonstration of feeling, people may wonder if you actually believe in the position you're championing.

Perhaps more important, however, is that effective persuaders have a strong and accurate sense of their audience's emotional state, and they adjust the tone of their arguments accordingly. Sometimes that means coming on strong, with forceful points. Other times, a whisper may be all that is required. The idea is that whatever your position, you match your emotional fervor to your audience's ability to receive the message.

Effective persuaders seem to have a second sense about how their colleagues have interpreted past events in the organization and how they will probably interpret a proposal. The best persuaders in our study would usually canvass key individuals who had a good pulse on the mood and emotional expectations of those about to be persuaded. They would ask those individuals how various proposals might affect colleagues on an emotional level—in essence, testing possible reactions. They were also quite effective at gathering information through informal conversations in the hallways or at lunch. In the end, their aim was to ensure that the emotional appeal behind their persuasion matched what their audience was already feeling or expecting.

To illustrate the importance of emotional matchmaking in persuasion, consider this example. The president of an aeronautics manufacturing company strongly believed that the maintenance costs and turnaround time of the company's U.S. and foreign competitors were so much better than his own company's that it stood to lose customers and profits. He wanted to communicate his fear and his urgent desire for change to his senior managers. So one afternoon, he called them into the boardroom. On an overhead screen was the projected image of a smiling man flying an old-fashioned biplane with his scarf blowing in the wind. The right half of the transparency was covered. When everyone was seated, the president explained that he felt as this pilot did, given the company's recent good fortune. The organization, after all, had just finished its most successful year in history. But then with a deep sigh, he announced that his happiness was quickly vanishing. As the president lifted the remaining portion of the sheet, he revealed an image of the pilot flying directly into a wall. The president then faced his audience and in a heavy voice said, "This is what I see happening to us." He asserted that the company was headed for a crash if people didn't take action fast. He then went on to lecture the group about the steps needed to counter this threat.

The reaction from the group was immediate and negative. Directly after the meeting, managers gathered in small clusters in the hallways to talk about the president's "scare tactics." They resented what they perceived to be the president's overstatement of the case. As the managers saw it, they had exerted enormous effort that year to break the company's records in sales and profitability. They were proud of their achievements. In fact, they had entered the meeting expecting it would be the moment of recognition. But to their absolute surprise, they were scolded.

The president's mistake? First, he should have canvassed a few members of his senior team to ascertain the emotional state of the group. From that, he would have learned that they were in need of thanks and recognition. He should then have held a separate session devoted simply to praising the team's accomplishments. Later, in a second meeting, he could have expressed his own anxieties about the coming year. And rather than blame the team for ignoring the future, he could have calmly described what he saw as emerging threats to the company and then asked his management team to help him develop new initiatives.

Now let us look at someone who found the right emotional match with his audience: Robert Marcell, head of Chrysler's small-car design team. In the early 1990s, Chrysler was eager to produce a new subcompact—indeed, the company had not introduced a new model of this type since 1978. But senior managers at Chrysler did not want to go it alone. They thought an alliance with a foreign manufacturer would improve the car's design and protect Chrysler's cash stores.

Marcell was convinced otherwise. He believed that the company should bring the design and production of a new subcompact in-house. He knew that persuading senior managers would be difficult, but he also had his own team to contend with. Team members had lost their confidence that they would ever again have the opportunity to create a good car. They were also angry that the United States had once again given up its position to foreign competitors when it came to small cars.

Marcell decided that his persuasion tactics had to be built around emotional themes that would touch his audience. From innumerable conversations around the company, he learned that many people felt as he did—that to surrender the subcompact's design to a foreign manufacturer was to surrender the company's soul and, ultimately, its ability to provide jobs. In addition, he felt deeply that his organization was a talented group hungry for a challenge and an opportunity to restore its self-esteem and pride. He would need to demonstrate his faith in the team's abilities.

Marcell prepared a 15-minute talk built around slides of his hometown, Iron River, a now defunct mining town in Upper Michigan, devastated, in large part, by foreign mining companies. On the screen flashed recent photographs he had taken of his boarded-up high school, the shuttered homes of his childhood friends, the crumbling ruins of the town's ironworks, closed churches, and an abandoned railroad yard. After a description of each of these places, he said the phrase, "We couldn't compete"—like the refrain of a hymn. Marcell's point was that the same outcome awaited Detroit if the production of small cars was not brought back to the United States. Surrender was the enemy, he said, and devastation would follow if the group did not take immediate action.

Marcell ended his slide show on a hopeful note. He spoke of his pride in his design group and then challenged the team to build a "made-in-America" subcompact that would prove that the United States could still compete. The speech, which echoed the exact sentiments of the audience, rekindled the group's fighting spirit. Shortly after the speech, group members began drafting their ideas for a new car.

Marcell then took his slide show to the company's senior management and ultimately to Chrysler chairman Lee Iacocca. As Marcell showed his slides, he could see that Iacocca was touched. Iacocca, after all, was a fighter and a strongly patriotic man himself. In fact, Marcell's approach was not too different from Iacocca's earlier appeal to the United States Congress to save Chrysler. At the end of the show, Marcell stopped and said, "If we dare to be different, we could be the reason the U.S. auto industry survives. We could be the reason our kids and grandkids don't end up working at fast-food chains." Iacocca stayed on for two hours as Marcell explained in greater detail what his team was planning. Afterward, Iacocca changed his mind and gave Marcell's group approval to develop a car, the Neon.

With both groups, Marcell skillfully matched his emotional tenor to that of the group he was addressing. The ideas he conveyed resonated deeply with his largely Midwestern audience. And rather than leave them in a depressed state, he offered them hope, which was more persuasive than promising doom. Again, this played to the strong patriotic sentiments of his American-heartland audience.

No effort to persuade can succeed without emotion, but showing too much emotion can be as unproductive as showing too little. The important point to remember is that you must match your emotions to your audience's.

The Force of Persuasion

The concept of persuasion, like that of power, often confuses and even mystifies businesspeople. It is so complex—and so dangerous when mishandled—that many would rather just avoid it altogether. But like power, persuasion can be a force for enormous good in an organization. It can pull people together, move ideas forward, galvanize change, and forge constructive solutions. To do all that, however, people must understand persuasion for what it is—not convincing and selling but learning and negotiating. Furthermore, it must be seen as an art form that requires commitment and practice, especially as today's business contingencies make persuasion more necessary than ever.

Originally published in May 1998. Reprint 98304

The Science of Pep Talks

by Daniel McGinn

ERICA GALOS ALIOTO stands in front of 650 sales reps in the New York office of Yelp, the online review company, wearing a pair of shiny gold pants that she calls her lucky LDOM pants. LDOM is Yelp's acronym for "last day of the month," and for Alioto, senior vice president for local sales, it means giving a speech that will motivate her sales force to cold-call 70 potential customers each and close deals before the accountants finalize that month's books.

She speaks for 20 minutes, extolling the group for being Yelp's top sales producer. She namechecks the best performers on the team and suggests ways for everyone else to adopt the same mentality. She tells stories. She asks questions.

"This office is currently $1.5 million away from target this month. . . . We have an action plan here. Are we going to execute?" There's moderate applause. She asks again, in a louder voice: *"Are we going to execute?"* Big applause.

Alioto has worked hard to perfect these speeches because she knows her success depends on them. Indeed, the ability to deliver an energizing pep talk that spurs employees to better performance is a prerequisite for any business leader. And yet few managers receive formal training in how to do it. Instead, they learn mostly from mimicry—emulating inspirational bosses, coaches they had in school, or even characters from films such as *Glengarry Glen Ross* and *The Wolf of Wall Street*. Some people lean on executive coaches for help, but often the advice rests on the coaches' personal experience, not research.

There is, however, a science to motivating people in this way. To better understand the various tools that help people get psyched up in the moments before important performances, I talked extensively with academics and practitioners in business and a variety of other fields. I discovered that while every individual has his or her own tips and tricks, according to the science, most winning formulas include three key elements: direction giving, expressions of empathy, and meaning making. The most extensive research in this field—dubbed motivating language theory, or MLT—comes from Jacqueline and Milton Mayfield, a husband-and-wife team at Texas A&M International University who have studied its applications in the corporate world for nearly three decades. Their findings are backed by studies from sports psychologists and military historians. And all the evidence suggests that once leaders understand these three elements, they can learn to use them more skillfully.

Three Elements, Carefully Balanced

The Mayfields describe direction giving as the use of "uncertainty-reducing language." This is when leaders provide information about precisely *how* to do the task at hand by, for example, giving easily understandable instructions, good definitions of tasks, and detail on how performance will be evaluated.

"Empathetic language" shows concern for the performer as a human being. It can include praise, encouragement, gratitude, and acknowledgment of a task's difficulty. Phrases like "How are we all doing?" "I know this is a challenge, but I trust you can do it," and "Your well-being is one of my top priorities" all fit into this category.

"Meaning-making language" explains why a task is important. This involves linking the organization's purpose or mission to listeners' goals. Often, meaning-making language includes the use of stories—about people who've worked hard or succeeded in the company, or about how the work has made a real difference in the lives of customers or the community.

Idea in Brief

The ability to deliver an energizing pep talk is a prerequisite for any business leader. But few managers receive formal training in how to give one. Instead, they learn mostly by emulating inspirational bosses, coaches, or even fictional characters.

However, research shows there is a science to psyching people up for better performance. According to motivating language theory, most winning formulas include three key elements: direction giving, or describing precisely how to do the task at hand; expressions of empathy, or concern for the performer; and meaning-making language, which explains why the task is important.

All the evidence suggests that, once leaders understand these three elements, they can learn to use them more skillfully.

A good pep talk—whether delivered to one person or many—should include all three elements, but the right mix will depend on the context and the audience. Experienced workers who are doing a familiar task may not require much direction. Followers who are already tightly bonded with a leader may require less empathetic language. Meaning making is useful in most situations, but may need less emphasis if the end goals of the work are obvious.

For example, the Mayfields studied the CEO of a California pharmaceutical start-up focused on drugs to alleviate heart disease and amyotrophic lateral sclerosis (ALS). Many of the company's employees have lost loved ones to these ailments, so they bring an unusual sense of purpose to their work. As a result, at all-hands meetings, the CEO can easily make statements like this: "I know everybody here wants to help save lives and make people's lives better. That's what our work is all about."

In contrast, the supervisor of a fast-food restaurant speaking to part-time teenage employees will need to work harder to incorporate all three elements of motivating language theory into his chats with staff, but he can't rely solely on direction giving. Milton Mayfield suggests empathetic lines: "I know this work is difficult; you go home every night smelling of grease, and you're working so late that you're up until midnight finishing your homework." Or, to creatively link labor to purpose, the supervisor might say: "Our goal as a company isn't just to provide people with fast, satisfying meals; it's also to provide good, stable jobs so that employees like you have money to help your families, to save for college, or to enjoy yourselves when you're not at work. The more you help this restaurant meet its goals, the better we'll be able to continue doing that." According to the Mayfields' research, meaning making is almost always the most difficult of the three elements to deliver.

Research from other fields offers additional insight into what gives the best pep talks their power. Tiffanye Vargas, a sports psychology professor at California State University at Long Beach, has published a half-dozen lab and field studies exploring which types of speeches best motivate athletes in different situations, some of which may also be applicable to business contexts. Her research suggests that across a variety of sports, coaches' pregame remarks do matter: 90% of players say they enjoy listening, and 65% say the speeches affect the way they play. She's found that people prefer an information-rich (uncertainty-reducing) speech if they're playing an unknown opponent or a team to which they've narrowly lost in the past. (For example: "We're going to beat this team with tough man-to-man coverage. Joe, your job is to neutralize that shooting guard; Jimmy, you box out that star rebounder on every play.") If a team is an underdog or playing in a high-stakes game, a more emotional pep talk (with more empathetic and meaning-making language) is more effective. (For example: "We've exceeded all expectations in this tournament. No one expects us to win. But *I* expect you to win. I know you can win. You have to win. For your teammates, for the fans—because you deserve this victory.")

Military speeches also tend to use the three elements of MLT in varying proportions, even if the terminology is different. When Keith Yellin, a former officer in the U.S. Marine Corps and the author of *Battle Exhortation: The Rhetoric of Combat Leadership,* analyzed precombat speeches dating back to the ancient Greeks and Romans (including literary accounts, such as the "Once more unto the breach" oratory in Shakespeare's *Henry V*), he found 23 "common topics" that generals call on. These include language that qualifies as direction giving ("Follow the plan"), but most of the themes appeal to soldiers' reason (by comparing their superior army to opponents' weaker forces) or emotions (by saying God is on their side or by highlighting the evilness of the enemy). Since the soldiers are about to risk their lives, it makes sense that a commander would focus on the larger purpose of the battle and why the risk is worthwhile.

At the same time, Yellin acknowledges that precombat oratory is less common today than in earlier wars, and its balance of elements has shifted. That's partly because today's armies are stealthy (limiting opportunities for speeches), but it's also because they're now more professionalized, made up mostly of career soldiers who voluntarily enlisted, rather than civilian soldiers or draftees. While new recruits might still benefit from rah-rah pep talks, seasoned soldiers already know their purpose and don't need as much empathy.

Stanley McChrystal, the retired four-star general who oversaw special operations in Iraq and Afghanistan, echoes this view. "If you went out with Delta Force or the Rangers or the SEALS in this last war, we were fighting every night," he says. "Stuff is happening so fast, they're all business." Earlier in his career, however, when he was leading younger soldiers, he relied more on emotion and meaning: "During the last 30 minutes or so [before a mission], it was more about building the confidence and the commitment to each other." He says he tended to start with direction giving ("Here's what I'm asking you to do") but quickly shifted to meaning making ("Here's why it's important") and empathy ("Here's why I know you can do it" and "Think about what you've done together before"), and then ended with a recap ("Now let's go and do it").

The upshot of all this research and anecdotal evidence is that leaders in any context need to understand each element of motivating language theory and be conscious of emphasizing the right one at the right time.

Putting Theory Into Practice

Alioto, the Yelp sales leader, has never studied the Mayfields' work, but she seems to have adopted the framework on her own. She leads with empathy—thanking the entire team for its hard work, singling

Grading a Sales Leader's Pep Talk

HBR ASKED MILTON AND JACQUELINE MAYFIELD to evaluate how well Yelp sales leader Erica Galos Alioto used motivating language theory with her team. They highlighted the three elements—<u>underlined for direction-giving language</u>, *italic for empathetic language*, and **bold for meaning-making language**—and offered comments on her approach. Edited excerpts follow.

Let me just say how impressed I am with this group. . . . Thank you for being the top office in Yelp right now, and for welcoming me with such incredible energy.

Right now the New York office is leading the company with 104% of quota, and there are two days left in the month. That's absolutely insane. . . . Colleen is at $80,000. I tried to say hello to her yesterday, but she was on the phone, pitching like a madwoman, so I couldn't. . . .[1]

Everybody knows how amazing the last day of the month is in the New York office. **But LDOM isn't really about the day of the month. It's about how we approach that day. There's something about that particular day that makes us come in with the ridiculous amount of grit and determination, the ability to make the unthinkable happen,**[2] the energy to achieve just about anything so that *no matter where we are in relation to quota, we're going to win. All those people who've been telling us no all month long—we're going to turn that around and get a yes. . . .*[3]

<u>Hopefully everybody has a pen and paper. I want you all to take a moment and write down what success looks like for you today. It may be how many business owners you talked to, or how many hearts and minds you won. . . . Write it down.</u>[4]

When you woke up this morning, what was your mentality? *Sometimes we get into negative self-talk. Sometimes it may sound like this: "Why is Jon at*

out people or small teams who've been crushing it, and emphasizing that if one Yelp salesperson can put up spectacular numbers, all the reps are capable of it, since they have similar skills and training. After reading a transcript of her talk, the Mayfields point to this line in particular: "No matter what's happened to you up to this point in the month, you can make it a successful day." Then she shifts to direction giving, offering insight on a basic informational concept— often dealing with having the right mindset or a commitment to act.

target today? He must have a really great territory." Sometimes we believe if
somebody is achieving something that we're not, it must be because the other
person has some advantage.[5]

Guess what? We also have plenty of examples of what people think of as a
bad territory, and we put somebody new on it, and they go out and absolutely
crush it.

If there's anything negative in your thinking, I encourage you to turn that
thinking on its head. Instead of looking at the differences between you and
somebody else with a lot of success, look for similarities.[6]

We've got two days to make it happen. **Everything you do today, every
action you take to make that successful outcome, every time you pitch,
every business owner you talk to, every time you encourage a teammate
to be better, every time you win the heart and mind of a business owner,
you're not only helping yourself—you're helping your team, you're helping your office, you're helping your company, and you're helping Yelp get
where it wants to be.[7]**

1. Praising the group and individual contributors
2. Portraying LDOM as a transcendent event and connecting the reps' actions to a
   larger goal
3. Acknowledging that some people are lagging, but emphasizing their self-efficacy
   and resilience
4. Offering specific guidance on how to approach the day's task
5. Recognizing employees' tendency to get discouraged, rather than be embold-
   ened, by colleague's success
6. Instructing reps to avoid negativity
7. Connecting today's work to the company's larger goal

For example, she tells the reps to write one goal for the day on a Post-
it and stick it on their computer.

Alioto ends with meaning making—an emotional rallying cry that
connects LDOM to a bigger goal and leaves the group energized:
"Every time you win the heart and mind of a business owner, you're
not only helping yourself—you're helping your team, you're helping your office, you're helping your company, and you're helping
Yelp get where it wants to be." The Mayfields note that she could

have gone a step further by connecting sales reps' work to how Yelp improves end users' lives by giving them access to recommendations and reviews of restaurants and other businesses. But on the whole, they give high marks to Alioto's use of rhetoric to motivate a sales team.

It's important to note, however, that Alioto's instruction, empathy, and meaning making don't stop when the salespeople file back to their desks. After her speech, she walks the sales floor, talking individually with more than a hundred reps and continuing to employ the different elements from motivating language theory. In one conversation, she talks to a rep about how to more forcefully close an ambivalent prospect. With a salesperson about to call an automobile mechanic, she talks about the specifics of that category. In other conversations, she tries to boost reps' confidence or emphasize the team's goals.

By day's end, the New York Yelpers have sold $1.45 million in new ads, meeting their quota and falling just $50,000 short of that month's stretch target. Many individual reps achieve their BME, Yelp-speak for "best month ever."

It's impossible to say how much her morning remarks and one-on-one talks influenced those results, but Alioto felt the day was successful. "My speech wasn't anything groundbreaking, but it helped them think about where they are and what they are capable of in a different way," she says. "I try to make everyone understand that they have the power to control their day."

Originally published in July–August 2017. Reprint R1704L

Get the Boss to Buy In

by Susan J. Ashford and James R. Detert

AN ENGINEERING MANAGER at an energy company—we'll call him John Healy—wanted to sell his boss on a safer and cheaper gas-scrubbing technology. This might have been an easy task if his boss, the general manager, hadn't selected the existing system just a year before. Instead it was, in Healy's words, "a delicate process." Fortunately, user reviews of the new technology had become available only in the past several months, which Healy tactfully mentioned in his presentation to the GM and other senior executives. He also included a detailed comparison of the two systems, drawing on implementations at comparable plants; the data suggested that the new system would remove contaminants more efficiently and reduce costs by about $700,000 a year. Because the GM was still on the fence, Healy brought in a bio-gas expert his boss trusted and respected to talk about the new technology's merits. The company made the investment and adopted the new system.

Organizations don't prosper unless managers in the middle ranks, like Healy, identify and promote the need for change. People at that level gather valuable intelligence from direct contact with customers, suppliers, and colleagues. They're in a position to see when the market is ripe for a certain offering, for instance, or to detect early signs that a partnership won't work out. But for many reasons, ranging from a fear of negative consequences to compliance with a top-down culture, they may not voice their ideas and concerns. As we know from our research and others' work in this area, not to mention recent news stories, such silence can have dire consequences—like "regulatory capture" in banking and un-checked product safety risks.

Even when they do speak up, most managers struggle to sell their ideas to people at the top. They find it difficult to raise issues to a "strategic" level early in the decision-making process—if they gain entry into such conversations at all. Studies show that senior executives dismiss good ideas from below far too often, largely for this reason: If they don't already perceive an idea's relevance to organizational performance, they don't deem it important enough to merit their attention. Middle managers have to work to alter that perception.

Their task is easier if certain contextual factors are in place—for instance, a track record of strong individual contributions, which enhances credibility, and a culture in which it's safe to speak up. Whether or not those stars are aligned, managers can improve their odds of success by using powerful methods of persuasion. Consider John Healy's approach: He presented his idea with emotional intelligence (making sure the GM didn't look bad for buying the current system), supported it with strong evidence from similar companies, and brought in a carefully chosen outside expert to bolster his argument.

Since Jane Dutton and Susan Ashford (a coauthor of this article) introduced the concept of "issue selling" into the academic discourse, more than two decades ago, many studies have proposed tactics for effectively winning support for new ideas. In a recent study of our own, we examined what actually works in organizations, across a range of roles and industries. Our participants described their experiences selling three basic types of ideas: new products, processes, markets, or customers to pursue; improvements to existing products or processes; and ways of better meeting employees' needs.

Issue sellers who accomplish their goals, we found, look for the best ways, venues, and times to voice their ideas and concerns—using rhetorical skill, political sensitivity, and interpersonal connections to move the right leaders to action. In particular, they employ seven tactics significantly more often than people who don't succeed in gaining buy-in. In this article we pull those tactics into a practical framework that managers can use to gain traction for their ideas, and we illustrate

Idea in Brief

The Problem

Middle managers glean valuable insights from their contact with customers, suppliers, and colleagues—but they struggle to sell their ideas to decision makers at the top. As a result, their organizations fail to seize opportunities and solve problems.

The Solution

Research shows that managers who gain buy-in from senior executives use seven tactics more often than managers whose ideas don't go anywhere.

The Benefits

These tactics provide a powerful framework for leading change from the middle ranks. By using them in an extended campaign for support, you can persuade senior leaders to take action and accomplish your goals.

them with examples from our research. Each tactic should be part of an extended campaign to win attention and resources.

Tactic 1: Tailor Your Pitch

More than any other tactic in our research sample, tailoring the pitch to decision makers was associated with success. It's essential for issue sellers to familiarize themselves with their audience's unique blend of goals, values, and knowledge and to allow that insight to shape their messages.

That's how one regional sales manager in the Canada division of an international oil company persuaded senior executives to restructure the sales organization and change its approach to attracting and motivating talent. Although sales teams in the oil industry are usually organized by customer, at this company each one covered a region. Because many customers had offices in multiple regions, teams often undermined one another's efforts by offering competing deals to the same clients. The organization's poor structure led to misaligned incentives and a fragmented customer experience. Making matters worse, most of the reps worked for salaries rather than commissions. "That's why a competitor managed to poach more than half my division's sales force," the regional manager said. Unsurprisingly, nearly

Middle Managers Are More Likely to Speak Up When They:

- Identify with the organization
- Have a positive relationship with their audience
- Feel psychologically safe in the organization
- Think someone above them will take action
- Care enough about the issue to invest energy in selling it

all the top performers had left. Having a sales structure so inefficient and out of touch with standard practices made such attrition practically inevitable. Although the executives who had created the structure were competent, they lacked sales experience. The remaining sales team, similarly, was technically knowledgeable but inexperienced, and the force was too small to sustain the business, let alone grow it.

When the regional manager initially shared his concerns with his boss and a few other executives, they disagreed, saying that the solution was simply to push people harder. "That sounded very risky to me, given that the division had just lost more than half its sales team," he told us. He made little progress until he asked other leaders in the division—those with greater decision-making power—what they expected from sales. He met with the new vice president of marketing and sales for Canada, for example, who wanted to prevent teams from working against one another and damaging credibility with clients.

In light of the feedback he'd gathered, the regional manager drafted recommendations and explained how they would help the division double revenue within four years (a target the CEO had recently announced to shareholders). Assigning sales teams to clients rather than to regions, he pointed out, would keep reps from stepping on one anothers' toes—which addressed the Canada VP's concerns. The manager also argued that attracting and retaining seasoned salespeople was essential to increasing revenue within the

CEO's desired time frame. He emphasized the division's high attrition rate for reps—about 40% walked out the door each year— and described how that could be fixed by following the industry's best practices for recruiting and managing sales talent. Commission-based compensation would attract experienced people and give them a reason to stay. Training would help greener reps develop important skills for managing customer relationships.

The Canada VP approved the plan and, more important, provided the resources to carry it out. "We added a dozen experienced people to the sales organization," the regional manager said. "And after implementation we had only one person leave in four years." That reduced the once-sizable turnover costs to almost nothing. The division also invested $75,000 in training, which more than paid for itself with a contest to see who could sell the most using the methods learned. (That alone brought $2.7 million in new business in one week.) Although the division missed its four-year target, it doubled revenue in five years.

In light of those benefits, executives no longer blamed laziness for the problems the sales force had experienced. And good people stopped leaving in droves, thanks partly to the shift in mindset at the top and partly to the improved structure and talent practices.

The regional manager attributed the inroads he made to his carefully tailored pitch. In addition to speaking directly to the Canada VP's and other leaders' goals, he said, "I had to show how my ideas could help meet the CEO's revenue expectations." That allowed him to move from one-on-one and small group meetings to a written proposal and a presentation he could share at a more senior level, where the initiatives got the support they needed.

Tactic 2: Frame the Issue

An issue's place on your organization's list of priorities depends heavily on how you package the idea. A new technological development might seem like techie trivia until you explain how it supports a strategic goal, such as increasing responsiveness to customers. It

Issue-Selling Prompts

THESE QUESTIONS WILL HELP YOU use the seven tactics effectively:

Tailor your pitch

- Where does my audience stand on this issue?

- What does my audience find most convincing or compelling?

Frame the issue

- How can I connect my issue to organizational priorities?

- How can I best describe its benefits?

- How can I link it to other issues receiving attention?

- How can I highlight an opportunity for the organization?

Manage emotions on both sides

- How can I use my emotions to generate positive rather than negative responses?

- How can I manage my audience's emotional responses?

Get the timing right

- What is the best moment to be heard? Can I "catch the wave" of a trend, for example, or tap into what's going on in the outside world?

- What is the right time in the decision-making process to raise my issue?

---

then becomes important. Once people see how your initiative fits into the big picture, they'll be more willing to devote resources to it.

Similarly, if you're a unit head presenting one of your directors to top management for promotion, you'll want to say that she exceeded her targets and spell out how she can contribute to key goals. You can describe how moving her into a more strategic role will help turn around a struggling department, for instance, or bring energy and creativity to a modestly performing part of the business. By framing her as a leader the organization needs instead of simply letting her impressive work speak for itself, you create a sense of urgency for decision makers. This isn't just someone who has accomplished a lot and deserves to advance, whenever and however that's convenient. It's someone with the skills and drive to make changes that matter now.

Involve others

- Which allies from my network can help me sell my issue, and how can I involve them effectively?

- Who are my potential blockers, and how can I persuade them to support me?

- Who are my fence-sitters, and how can I convince them that my issue matters?

Adhere to norms

- Should I use a formal, public approach to sell my issue (for example, a presentation to upper management)? Or an informal, private approach (casual one-on-one conversations)? Or a combination of the two?

Suggest solutions

- Am I suggesting a viable solution?

- If not, am I proposing a way to discover one instead of just highlighting the problem?

As these scenarios show, it's often effective to highlight an idea's business benefits; the successful sellers in our research took that approach significantly more often than those who'd failed. For example, a chief investment officer at a financial firm described how he very gradually made the case that subscribing to a proprietary real estate database was "a need and not just a want." Every six months or so, over a period of about five years, he would float the suggestion at a moment when access to the database would be useful, and a tech-savvy ally in the asset management department would vocally agree. But they needed broader support for the idea, because most people viewed it as a luxury. "We are a lean-running organization that has historically resisted adopting new technologies," the chief investment officer explained. Eventually he identified a relevant need in another part of the business: The database could help the accounting department meet its public-reporting and audit requirements. That was the tipping point. He'd spelled out the business benefits for multiple departments. The firm decided to subscribe.

Moral framing appears to be less powerful than business framing. In our research, the few instances of moral framing were associated with failed attempts or uneven results. When issue sellers peddle their principles too aggressively, people may react negatively to what they perceive as a judgment of their character.

Although focusing on business benefits is often safer, sellers may need to underscore the urgency. They might, for instance, present the idea as an opportunity that shouldn't be missed. Our successful sellers were significantly more likely than the others to explain what the organization stood to gain from their ideas. Emphasizing the positive can give your audience a sense of control over the situation and inspire optimism and buy-in.

Highlighting a threat—a consequence of not adopting your idea— can also create pressure to act. But it can backfire: When decision makers focus on potential loss, they sometimes then bury their heads and avoid the issue. The amount of threat framing did not differ between successful and unsuccessful selling attempts, perhaps because it was viewed as a mixed bag: It's hard to predict whether it will spur action—the classic "fight" response—or result in "flight."

Finally, issue sellers often find success by bundling their ideas with related ones. For instance, someone lobbying to increase leave time for employees caring for aging or sick family members might allude to efforts to increase parental leave. When attached to a larger initiative, a small idea can gain prominence. It's no longer just an elder-care issue; it's a work/life balance issue.

Tactic 3: Manage Emotions on Both Sides

Because issue selling is an interpersonal activity, often involving high stakes, it inevitably stirs emotions. Passion, if appropriately expressed, improves sellers' chances of gaining attention and triggering action. There's a fine line, however, between passion and anger. People sometimes propose initiatives because they are fed up with existing conditions or behavior. And as they encounter road-blocks to their selling efforts, their frustrations may intensify.

Though strong emotions can be channeled into a rousing appeal for action, when unregulated they're more likely to diminish the sell-er's influence. Decision makers who detect negative emotions from subordinates offering input tend to perceive those employees as com-plainers, not as change agents. Further, recent research by Wharton's Adam Grant shows that people who keep their emotions in check—or at least control what they display to others—feel more comfortable raising issues and receive higher performance evaluations.

Our study supports Grant's finding: Successful issue sellers paid much more attention to emotional regulation than those who failed. Indeed, the latter sometimes understood that their runaway emo-tions were partly to blame for their failures.

Important as self-regulation is, it's equally critical to under-stand and manage the decision maker's emotions—they, too, can make or break your case. John Healy, the manager in our opening example, did that especially well. Anticipating how his boss might feel about having selected the more hazardous and more expensive gas-scrubbing system, he was careful to point out that user reviews of the new technology hadn't been available when that decision had been made. Sellers hoping to have their issues heard should seek to inspire positive emotions in the decision makers—by focusing on benefits, for instance, or showing how action is possible. In our sample, successful sellers reported doing this far more often than others.

Tactic 4: Get the Timing Right

It's critical to find the right moment to raise your ideas. That moment might be when organizational priorities shift, when certain players leave or join the company, or when a boss's preoccupations change. Successful sellers in our study reported greater sensitivity than oth-ers to timing, by a wide margin. The best sellers notice when more and more people are beginning to care about a larger topic or trend that's related to their issue, and they position their idea to "catch the wave."

For example, the managing director of an Ecuadoran holding company's luxury division chose just the right time to persuade his CFO and board to tap an unexplored market in Peru. He'd gotten the idea in 2007. Though it was a viable option then, he held off on proposing it, given Peru's recent civil unrest and the fact that his division still had room for growth in its home market. In 2009, after the recession, "Peru had the best-performing stock market in the world," the director said. So his team took a trip to assess the potential. "We looked at new construction developments, and the modern minimalism was in stark contrast with the high-walled constructions from the guerrilla and terrorist era." It seemed that Peru was not just doing well but primed for growth. "There was only one prominent shopping mall, and 'hard' luxury items such as designer-branded bags, watches, and sunglasses were scarce or sold informally," he explained. "Yet Starbucks cafés were full every day and expanding." The director and his team decided that a luxury boutique carrying various products but focusing on watches would be the best project to pursue. They knew that department stores wouldn't cover the demand, because customers would want the luxury experience. "We thought Peru was ready for it," he said. The timing was excellent for another reason: The market in Ecuador had become saturated by then.

The director got the approval he needed, and the company opened two luxury stores in November 2010. "The day we opened our first boutique we sold the entire inventory of perfume we had bought from the pharmacy next door," he said. "One customer came in and bought all our stock of ink for his luxury writing instrument out of fear of not finding the ink again." That store accounted for 40% of the division's profits over the following three years. By 2011 all the most prestigious luxury brands had entered the Peruvian market—but this company had gotten there first.

In addition to keeping a close eye on larger trends and events, it's important to be mindful of deadlines. If an idea relates directly to an imminent product launch or software release, by all means speak up—now is the time to be heard. But as recent research shows, when a deadline is far away and decision makers are still in exploration mode, open-ended inquiry can be more effective than proposing a specific solution. Of course, sellers can't always know their audiences' deadlines. If you discover an immediate challenge, though, you can try to address it in your proposal—and shelve other ideas until people have time to really think them through.

Tactic 5: Involve Others

Issue sellers usually are better off bringing others into their efforts than going it alone. Building a coalition generates organizational buy-in more quickly and on a larger scale as more people contribute energy and resources. One person might have access to important data, for example, and another might have a personal relationship with one of the top managers you're trying to persuade. Perhaps recognizing these advantages, our successful respondents were more likely than the others to involve colleagues in pitching their ideas.

Negotiation experts would tell you to mobilize your allies, persuade your blockers to support the issue or at least back off, and show the fence-sitters why they should care about your idea. When building a coalition, you can reach out to experts in relevant areas to add to your credibility, though a recent study of reactions to issue sellers suggests that it's just as important to include individuals the target audience trusts. Certainly tap members of your network, but also involve people whose networks don't overlap with yours. That will expand the pool of people who might advocate for your idea or lend their expertise.

Tactic 6: Adhere to Norms

The tactics we've covered so far draw on two types of knowledge that successful issue sellers need: strategic (understanding the organization's goals, the plans to achieve them, and the roles decision makers play in those efforts) and relational (figuring out who will be affected by your issue, who cares about it, who might object to it, and so on). Here we'll discuss a third type: knowledge of organizational norms, such as what kinds of data your leaders like to use to make decisions, how they prefer to receive information, and whether they tend to get behind issues similar to yours. Grasping such norms can give you a sense of how effective the other tactics described in this article will be. For example, a study of employees selling environmental issues found that the use of drama and emotion worked only if the organization already had a strong environmental commitment.

One important norm to understand is whether it's generally best to use formal or informal approaches. Casual conversations allow issue sellers to get an off-the-record read on their ideas and avoid putting their target audience on the spot in public. But formal approaches can convey seriousness and apply helpful pressure on decision makers to respond. Issue sellers need to consider these trade-offs in light of what's expected in their organizations. In one company we studied, senior managers claimed to want innovative thinking but were described, even at "blue sky" meetings, as chastising those who didn't present slide shows using company-approved templates. Not surprisingly, their employees reported selling in very formal ways while acknowledging the dampening effect this probably had on innovation.

Successful sellers used more formal—and fewer informal—tactics than those whose pitches failed. So it seems that many business settings require a certain level of convention and decorum, and that the best sellers adapt their behavior to fit that norm. Our qualitative data suggests that sequencing matters, though: People who succeeded tended to roll out their ideas informally early on, in order to gauge interest, and then switch to formal presentations.

Tactic 7: Suggest Solutions

Clearly, people believe that if they're going to speak up about problems, they'd better suggest thoughtful fixes: This was the most frequently used tactic among both types of sellers, successful and not. And those who succeeded used it significantly more often than those who didn't. They pointed to specific solutions, such as adding a business operations team to address a systems flaw. They often included funding ideas when selling the need for something new.

Proposing a solution signals that the seller has put thought into the issue and respects leaders' time. Indeed, recent laboratory research shows that people think more highly of issue sellers who suggest solutions.

But here's the hitch: If people are less likely to raise issues for which they haven't identified a solution, as our data shows, organizations where problems crop up faster than people can devise fixes are at a considerable disadvantage. What's more, some problems are best solved by a group of people who bring diverse knowledge, experience, and expertise to the table. In these cases, expecting issue sellers to have solutions in hand may lead to poor decision making.

Sellers who feel strongly about an issue but don't see a solution can suggest a sensible process for discovering one. That way they follow the norm of being solution-focused while getting others constructively involved in a timely manner.

Create a Tactical Campaign

There's more to a pitch than a big presentation and a yea-or-nay decision. Those are just the most visible steps in the process. Leading up to them, you should carefully lay a foundation for your argument, tactic by tactic, as you acquire resources and knowledge. Here are some principles to help you make the most of the tactics we've described.

Choose your battles

Some ideas are just plain tough to sell—those that are too far ahead of the audience's current understanding, for instance, or too much of a stretch beyond the organization's norms. That's especially true of any idea that may seem an indictment of the status quo or, worse, of the audience's intelligence, judgment, or morality. In such cases, you may have an uphill battle no matter how skillfully you frame the issue and manage emotions.

Even the best issue sellers can't win every time, and sometimes the payoff isn't worth the effort. To determine whether to invest resources and social capital in selling an issue, ask two questions: How important is this to my company? And how important is it to me? That will help you assess how much risk to take on. Raising concerns about a company's approach to foreign labor practices or about managers' treatment of employees will probably elicit much more pushback than ideas for enhancing products or improving processes. But if the former issues are critical to the organization's well-being or your own professional identity, you might sensitively pursue them even if you know you won't succeed in the short term.

Combine tactics

In our regression analysis, we found that campaigns using multiple tactics succeeded more often than those using any single tactic. Indeed, the combined use of all seven tactics accounted for about 40% of the difference between successes and failures. We saw the same kind of impact in individuals' descriptions of their selling efforts. The engineering manager at the energy company managed the GM's emotions, suggested a solution backed by data, and turned to an outside expert for further support. The Ecuadoran managing director also combined tactics: In addition to choosing the right moment to launch the luxury goods stores, he adhered to his conservative organization's norms for proposing projects—starting with informal conversations, looking at proxy businesses in other industries (in this case, Starbucks), talking with customers and partners to gather insights, and finally building up to the formal review process, using traditional financial tools and outsourced market studies for analysis.

Approach the right audience

It's a common dilemma: Should you air your idea with your boss and risk getting nowhere because he or she lacks sufficient power or interest to back you up? Or go straight to decision makers who will care—and quite likely pay a price for bypassing your manager? Wishing to avoid trouble, many sellers start with their boss and hope their ideas make their way up the hierarchy. But their issues often die right away or languish until senior management becomes aware of them. Sometimes the immediate boss doesn't even bother escalating the issue; other times the messenger isn't as skilled as the initial seller at making the case.

So ask if you can accompany anyone selling on your behalf, whether that's your manager or a colleague who has an "in" with a formal decision-making body. If that's not possible, do everything you can to prepare that person to sell effectively: Work out the details of the business case, help identify the right time and venue for presenting it, and so forth. If you decide to approach decision makers directly, keep your boss in the loop. Otherwise you'll need to have a very good answer when senior leaders ask why you've come to them instead of to your manager.

No set of prescriptions can capture the nuances of every environment or remove the risks and disappointments of issue selling. But sellers who routinely and effectively use these tactics enjoy greater success than those who don't.

Issue selling isn't a discrete event; it's an ongoing process that requires groundwork, pacing, and patience. When midlevel managers do it effectively, their ideas get decision makers' attention and make a real difference.

Originally published in January–February 2015. Reprint R1501E

The Organizational Apology

by Maurice E. Schweitzer, Alison Wood Brooks, and Adam D. Galinsky

THE *WASHINGTON POST* called it "creepy." The *Atlantic* said it "might have been illegal." One privacy advocate wondered if it could have made people suicidal.

Those were just some of the reactions to the disclosure, in June 2014, that Facebook had allowed academic researchers to manipulate the news feeds of 689,000 users for one week. The experiment, in which half of the users saw fewer positive posts than usual and the other half saw fewer negative ones than usual, was designed to determine whether the changes would cause people to write more positive or negative posts themselves. In fact, the researchers did find evidence of "emotional contagion" and published the results in a prestigious scientific journal. But their findings were eclipsed by the public outcry.

Shortly after the story broke, the lead researcher issued a statement saying that he and his colleagues were sorry for the anxiety their work had caused. But Facebook defended its actions for days, explaining that the boilerplate language in its 9,000-word user agreement constituted informed consent. Nearly a week elapsed before the company's chief operating officer offered a half-hearted apology for "poorly communicating" about the study. Three months later, the chief technology officer issued another statement, saying Facebook had been "unprepared for the reaction," conceding, "there are things we should have done differently," and articulating new research guidelines. Still, he avoided the words "sorry" and "apologize."

In this episode, Facebook erred in two ways: First, it violated users' trust. Second, it compounded the problem with an awkward, three-step, not-very-contrite apology.

Scenarios like this are all too common. At some point, every company makes a mistake that requires an apology—to an individual; a group of customers, employees, or business partners; or the public at large. And more often than not, organizations and their leaders fail to apologize effectively, if at all, which can severely damage their relationships with stakeholders and their reputations, especially if the incidents become public (and publicized).

Companies need clear guidelines for determining whether a misstep merits an apology and, when it does, how to deliver the message. In this article, we present an apology formula, drawn from our work and research in management and psychology, that provides a diagnostic and practical guidance on the who, what, where, when, and how of an effective apology. The bottom line for serious transgressions: Senior leaders must immediately express candor, remorse, and a commitment to change in a high-profile setting—and make it sincere.

The Apology Dilemma

Let's recognize two facts about apologies at the outset: First, we are psychologically predisposed to find reasons (or excuses) to delay or avoid saying we're sorry. Apologizing feels uncomfortable and risky. There's a loss of power or face involved—it rearranges the status hierarchy and makes us beholden, at least temporarily, to the other party. That doesn't feel good. So it's no wonder people try to avoid dwelling on or drawing attention to mistakes and that when one is pointed out, they get defensive, arguing their side of the story and shifting blame to others.

Apologies are even more difficult in an organizational context. When considering whether and how to apologize, even seasoned leaders can become gripped by indecision. That's understandable. A company mistake is often caused by a single division or employee,

Idea in Brief

The Problem

Organizations often struggle to get apologies right. Many leaders fear that an apology could expose their firm to legal action; others offer a cursory "I'm sorry" without addressing victims' concerns. Bungling an apology is costly, resulting in damaged reputations and relationships.

The Solution

Companies need clearer guidelines for determining whether a mistake merits an apology and, when it does, for crafting and delivering an effective message.

The Formula

Ask four questions: Was there a violation? Was it core to our promise or mission? How will the public react? Are we committed to change? Then think carefully about the who, what, where, when, and how of executing the apology.

and a bad situation is frequently made worse by events beyond its control. It can feel unjust for a CEO or an entire organization to have to take responsibility.

Second, companies have a strong tendency to evaluate the situation through a legal lens. Corporate counsel may fixate on whether any laws were broken and warn managers that an apology might be construed as an admission of liability (possibly exposing the company to litigation) rather than as an effort to empathize with the wronged party. This is an important distinction, because effective apologies address the recipients' feelings—they don't prove a point. Unfortunately, a litigious perspective has become ingrained in many organizations: Even a leader who isn't actively consulting with an attorney may worry that an apology could create legal problems.

Companies need to stop thinking this way. Most apologies are low cost—and many create substantial value. They can help defuse a tense situation, and fears of litigation are often unfounded. Consider health care providers. For many years, medical professionals were advised not to apologize when they made mistakes that hurt or even killed patients, because doing so might make the hospital vulnerable to a malpractice lawsuit. But research has revealed that when some hospitals began allowing doctors to offer apologies to patients and families, or even made apologizing mandatory, the likelihood of litigation was *reduced*.

Should You Apologize?

If a company is debating whether or not to apologize, managers should consider the nature and severity of the violation and the costs and benefits of offering an apology. Four questions can help determine if an apology is necessary.

1. Was there a violation, whether real or perceived?
When a company apologizes, it accepts full or partial blame for causing harm. So it needs to first determine whether a violation has in fact occurred and if so, whether the company is responsible. But here's the tricky part—this needs to be done quickly and perceptions of responsibility matter.

Consider the crisis Coca-Cola faced in 1999. It began on June 8, when a schoolboy in Belgium reported feeling ill after drinking a Coke. Within days, hundreds of people had attributed fevers, dizziness, and nausea to Coca-Cola beverages, and many made their way to hospitals. At first, the company insisted that its products did not pose a health risk and that bad carbon dioxide at a plant in Antwerp had triggered unnecessary alarm. CEO M. Douglas Ivester, hoping that the crisis would "blow over," said that he'd decided to "take a lower profile on this." But by the end of the week, the company was forced to remove more than 50 million beverages from the shelves in France, Germany, and Belgium. Finally, more than a week after the first incident, Ivester said publicly that he and his executives "deeply regret any problems encountered by our European consumers."

If we put ourselves in Ivester's shoes, we can easily understand why Coca-Cola might have had trouble making a quick decision about whether to apologize. First, we'd all prefer to see the results of an internal investigation and understand exactly what caused the bad outcome—and how to prevent it from happening again—before making any statements. Second, we'd be just as likely to hope that the issue would fade from attention. And third, we'd probably feel defensive and that we'd been unfairly blamed. The senior executives at Coca-Cola honestly believed that the reported health concerns were exaggerated and that many of the complaints had nothing to do with their products.

But companies must overcome the tendency to wait, to keep a low profile, or to argue the facts. Instead, leaders should consider others' perceptions of the potential violation and move swiftly to address them. An apology enables an executive to express concern and convey the organization's values—even as an investigation into exactly what happened and who was responsible unfolds.

As we make the apology decision, we need to consider the "psychological contract"—the expectations customers, employees, business partners, or other stakeholders have about an organization's responsibilities and what is right or fair. This often extends well beyond any explicit contract. To understand those expectations, managers have to imagine the situation from different vantage points.

Consider Mattel's launch of Hello Barbie, a doll that records and uploads conversations to Mattel online so that it can make personalized responses. Mattel thought that the doll's ability to remember a child's name and preferences would be a unique selling point, but critics quickly voiced privacy concerns. Mattel never intended to cause harm, but consumers' perceptions of an "eavesdropping Barbie" were so negative that it was forced to offer public reassurances to customers that Mattel was committed to safety and security. Presumably, leaders could have predicted that a toy that recorded children's play and uploaded it to the company would raise flags. In the Facebook situation, had the company considered the perspectives of its stakeholders before launching its emotion manipulation study, it might have avoided much of the fallout. And Coca-Cola should have known that even the perception of health concerns related to its products should be addressed immediately.

2. Was the violation core or noncore?

Certain activities and responsibilities are central to a company's products, services, and mission. Other responsibilities are peripheral or less consequential. If an automaker's vehicles contain a flaw that imperils drivers' safety or a restaurant's diners suffer food poisoning, those are core violations. When the accounting firm Arthur Andersen certified Enron's financial statements and failed to expose the company's massive fraud, it violated its core responsibility.

Other violations might involve a business function that's outside the company's operational core. For instance, Apple and other companies have been criticized for using transfer pricing and other financial tools to minimize their tax bills—a practice that offends people who see paying taxes as a civic duty. Although it constitutes a violation for at least some of their consumers, it is not core, because tax accounting is not those companies' central activity.

Core violations pose a fundamental threat to the mission of the organization. Therefore, a robust apology is critical—and a botched one can cause significant damage. A company that has committed a noncore violation has greater flexibility, though an apology may still be warranted or beneficial.

3. How will the public react?

Sometimes violations that harm only a single person or a small group can remain private matters. But remember, thanks to Twitter, Instagram, Yelp, Facebook, and other social media outlets, a single customer complaint can easily go viral and influence the perceptions of millions of potential customers. Even the smallest transgressions can blow up into epic (and costly) public relations nightmares.

Consider what happened to United Airlines in 2008. The company allegedly damaged a Canadian singer's guitar during a flight from Halifax to Nebraska and then subjected him to a Kafkaesque customer service experience. In the pre-internet era, the public would probably never have learned about the incident. Social media has changed that: In this case, the frustrated singer wrote a song called "United Breaks Guitars" and posted a video of it on YouTube. It became a sensation, with nearly 15,000 views its first day and more than 14 million since. Eventually, Rob Bradford, United's managing director of customer solutions, telephoned the singer and apologized directly; he also asked if the airline could use the video to help improve its customer service.

In gauging the probable reaction to an incident, companies should take into account the relative size and status of the parties. A violation committed by a large, powerful, or high-status organization (such as United, Google, Walmart, or the U.S. government) against a low-status, low-power person or group is more likely to engender public outrage—and require an apology—than a violation committed by a mom-and-pop business or one that hurts only wealthy individuals or corporations.

4. Is the company willing to commit to change?

In assessing whether or not to apologize, organizational leaders must also focus on the extent to which they are willing—and able—to change the company's behavior. If they can't or don't want to do things differently in the future, the case for making an apology is weak, because it will sound hollow and unconvincing.

When Target and Home Depot suffered cyber-security breaches that exposed customers' credit card information to hackers, the companies' apologies would have been ineffective without promises to institute procedures to prevent a reccurrence. (For a look at instances when it makes sense for companies to stand firm in the face of perceived harm, see the sidebar "The Power of Being Unapologetic.")

Sometimes managers become so focused on their new course of action that they forget to apologize. That's a mistake; without a show of remorse, people are likely to think you're whitewashing the violation.

The Apology Formula: The Right Way to Apologize

Once a company has decided that it should apologize, it has to do it right. It's astonishing how many well-intentioned, sophisticated organizations completely botch apologies. While a good apology can restore balance or even improve relationships, a bad apology can make things much worse. As a framework for getting it right, companies need to think carefully about who, what, where, when, and how.

Get Your Apology Right the First Time

Do Convey Remorse

"Today's GM will do the right thing. That begins with my sincere apologies to . . . the families and friends [of those] who lost their lives or were injured. I am deeply sorry."

—Mary Barra, CEO, GM, in 2014 testimony to the U.S. Congress in the wake of the company's ignition-switch recall

Don't Be Tone Deaf

"We're sorry for the massive disruption it's caused to [people's] lives. There's no one who wants this thing over more than I do. I want my life back."

—Tony Hayward, then CEP, BP, in 2010 after a rig explosion caused the biggest oil spill in U.S. history

Do Show Candor

"We've been doing a terrible job . . . meeting demand for our products. . . . We suck at this. I suck at this. I apologize to all of you. . . ."

—Min Liang-Tan, CEO, Razer, after missing the April 2014 shipping date for its gaming laptop

Don't Address the Wrong Victim

"I'm sad for the people of Lululemon who . . . had to face the brunt of my actions. I'm sorry to have put you all through this."

—Chip Wilson, Founder, Lululemon, in 2013, after blaming his company's see-through yoga pants fiasco on the women who wear them

Do Get the Message Out

"You count on us at JetBlue . . . and we know we let some of you down . . . and for that we are truly sorry."

—Rob Maruster, then-COO, JetBlue, in a 2011 YouTube apology to passengers who'd been stranded on the tarmac for nearly eight hours

---

Who

The more serious and the more core the violation, the more necessary it becomes that a senior leader—up to and including the CEO—make the apology. In cases where there is a clear transgressor— an employee who made the mistake—there may be merit in involving that person. But if he or she isn't sufficiently senior, you risk

The Power of Being Unapologetic

SOMETIMES AN UNAPOLOGETIC STANCE makes sense. Consider these examples:

- John Chambers, the former CEO of Cisco, was criticized for how he handled innovation at the company. He assembled teams to create small start-up companies that Cisco would later buy at predetermined prices—a practice that made some employees very wealthy and others extremely resentful. But Chambers wouldn't apologize, because he had a message to send: Innovation was more important to him than equitable pay.

- Although fast-food giant McDonald's has responded to concerns about the nutritional content of its food with more-healthful menus and smaller portion sizes, it took a new stance in a recent marketing campaign. Its ads unapologetically promote the Big Mac as "not Greek yogurt" and as a sandwich that "will never be kale."

When leaders and corporations embrace their values and identity—unapologetically—they stand to gain credibility and power.

---

offending the wronged party or the public by conveying that you are not taking the violation seriously. Just as it's better to be overdressed than underdressed, when in doubt, you should err on the side of having a senior executive offer the apology.

For example, Target released a statement from then-CEO Gregg Steinhafel the day after its security breach came to light. When a plane full of JetBlue passengers was stranded on a runway for eight hours, it was then-COO Rob Maruster who issued the apology on YouTube.

Deciding who should receive the apology is often straightforward—although companies can slip up here too. Consider the video that Chip Wilson, the founder of Lululemon, released during the furor over an interview in which he had said that his brand's yoga pants weren't suitable for some bodies. His "I'm sorry to have put you all through this" was addressed to employees, not customers, and was roundly criticized. Effective apologies are delivered directly to the person or people harmed. When that group is large and diffuse, the organization might want to offer an "open" apology through the press or social media.

What

This is the substance of the apology—the words you say and the actions you take. It's important to keep three goals in mind: candor, remorse, and a commitment to change.

The best apologies show *candor.* They leave no room for equivocation or misinterpretation, and they make absolutely clear that the organization acknowledges both the harm that was caused and its own responsibility. Consider the candid apology Razer's CEO gave after severe delays for preorders of the company's Blade laptop in 2014. "We've been doing a terrible job anticipating and meeting demand for our products . . . We suck at this. I suck at this. I apologize to all of you who have had to wait for ages each time we launch a new product."

Organizations should never sound defensive or as if they're trying to justify a violation. However, explanations and information can help. For instance, an airline's apology for a mechanical delay is more effective if the airline explains exactly what part is broken, what's being done to fix it, how much time it will take, and why the issue will pose no safety risk once fixed. Military condolence letters— a form of institutional apology—routinely offer details regarding the circumstances of the mission on which the soldier was killed. After receiving some information, those affected have a greater appreciation for the broader context and the institution's perspective.

Effective apologies also express *remorse.* We've criticized Facebook's handling of the emotion manipulation study, but in 2006, when users were upset by the company's just-launched News Feed feature, CEO Mark Zuckerberg offered a pitch-perfect apology. "We really messed this one up," his written statement began. He went on to use phrases like "bad job," "errors," "we missed this point," "big mistake," and "I'm sorry." He even thanked groups that had formed to protest. "Even though I wish I hadn't made so many of you angry, I am glad we got to hear you." His choice of words was remorseful and self-abasing—and effective.

The third key ingredient is demonstrating *a commitment to change.* An apology should create distance from the "old self" that committed the violation and establish a "new self" that will not engage in similar behavior. Sometimes the employee responsible for an error is fired. Sometimes, as in the Target and Home Depot security breaches, new procedures are put in place. Organizations might also demonstrate a seriousness of purpose by appointing an independent authority to investigate the incident and recommend changes—and pledging to implement the recommendations.

Consider how the Vancouver Taxi Association responded in 2014 after a cab driver left a mother and her sick child on the side of the road after he realized that they intended to pay for their ride from a local hospital to the airport with a hospital-issued taxi voucher, which he didn't believe his cab company would accept. (In fact it would.) Not only did the taxi association express remorse for the incident, it demonstrated a commitment to change by suspending the driver and instituting a clear policy instructing all cabs to accept all vouchers from local hospitals at all times.

Now let's consider an apology that lacked the three "what" elements: candor, remorse, and a commitment to change. In 2009, Goldman Sachs CEO Lloyd Blankfein issued a vague apology for unspecified acts by the financial industry that led to the Great Recession. His language was roundly criticized. As the *New York Times* editorialized, "His remarks do not come close to an apology . . . since he never actually said what he was sorry for . . . or to whom he was apologizing." Nor did he explain how the bank would change its behavior.

Blankfein learned his lesson, however. After this very public rebuke, he held another press conference, in which he admitted that Goldman had participated "in things that were clearly wrong and we have reasons to regret and apologize for." The firm pledged $500 million to help small businesses recover from the recession. This apology was far more candid, expressed remorse, and demonstrated a commitment to change.

Where

If a company wants to control the coverage of an apology, the setting can determine how loud—and widely heard—the message will be. Organizations often default to written statements that reach a broad audience, especially when they're published in newspapers. Target did this following its security breach, as did News International after some of its newspapers were found to have illegally hacked phones. For a more personal touch, the CEO or another executive might videotape an on-camera statement, as JetBlue's Maruster did. A live statement, with or without an audience, increases the perceived importance of the apology. In some instances, it may even make sense for leaders to travel to the place where the violation happened—a crash site, the location of an industrial accident, and so on. This not only provides a camera-ready backdrop, but also it shows that the executive cares enough to view the damage firsthand and apologize to victims in person. For example, when a Southwest Airlines flight overshot the runway at Chicago's Midway Airport in 2005, killing a six-year-old boy and injuring others, CEO Gary Kelly immediately flew to Chicago, visited the hospital, held a press conference, and offered several apologies, winning high marks for sensitivity.

Managers should realize, however, that there are risks to this approach. A live, on-site apology puts a leader in an uncontrolled environment. Apologizing to victims face-to-face can be effective if they accept the apology—but if they don't, the event could turn into a public confrontation. Sometimes public apologies come off as publicity stunts. Social media has changed the calculus for choosing where to make an apology, since now a company's written statement can be shared and retweeted, reaching many more people than would typically see an address on the evening news.

When

A good apology arrives quickly. Speed signals sincerity and dispels the idea that executives feel uncertainty or ambiguity about their responsibility. Sometimes, companies delay apologies for good reasons, such as Coke's desire, in 1999, to investigate customers' health concerns and their root cause. Facebook's intention to present a fully-formed plan to show its commitment to change appears to have been one factor in its slow apology for the emotion-manipulation study. The desire to be cautious is reasonable, but we believe that it's better to offer a quick "placeholder" apology than to be silent.

"While we're still gathering the facts to understand exactly what took place, we want our customers and employees to know that we apologize for any harm we have caused. Know that we are developing plans to ensure that this doesn't happen again. We will follow up by the end of the week with details."

While speedy apologies are preferable, the window of opportunity for apologizing never completely closes, and for many victims a belated apology is better than none at all. Consider the well-received statement made by GM's Mary Barra after the company's 2014 recall of faulty ignition switches—a problem the company had known about, but not acted on, for 10 years: "Today's GM will do the right thing . . . I am deeply sorry." Barra also told employees that the violation was "unacceptable"; 15 leaders deemed responsible for the cover-up were let go. If a previous CEO decided not to offer an apology for a violation but the new CEO believes one is warranted, the organization should make one regardless of the time lag.

How

The way an apology is delivered can matter just as much as the content of the apology. Informal language and personal communication can help. Recall Zuckerberg's use of the phrase "We really messed this one up."

Or consider what happened when DiGiorno pizza used the hashtag #WhyIStayed to promote its pizzas, not realizing that the tag was already being used by women to share their experiences of abuse. The company not only deleted its initial tweet but also followed it with another: "A million apologies. Did not read what the hashtag was about before posting." It sent direct tweets to every person who had expressed outrage: "@ejbrooks It was. And I couldn't be more sorry for it, Emma. Please accept my deepest apologies."

Written statements have the benefit of being broadcast quickly, but it is often easier to strike the right tone through speech. A leader can rely on nonverbal cues to convey emotion, humility, and empathy. For example, remorse can be shown through facial expressions, and a commitment to change reinforced through vigorous gestures.

But in-person apologies are tricky to master. It can be difficult for business leaders accustomed to displaying power and self-confidence to strike the right repentant tone. For some, it may require careful planning and rehearsal. One glaring example of a leader who got the "how" of his apology wrong is Tony Hayward, then-CEO of BP. During the catastrophic Deepwater Horizon oil spill, in the Gulf of Mexico, he delivered the following apology: "We're sorry for the massive disruption it's caused to [people's] lives. There's no one who wants this thing over more than I do. I'd like my life back." It was a strikingly tone-deaf remark, one that illustrates the danger of an off-the-cuff or improvised apology. (Hayward resigned a few weeks later.)

Preparing to Apologize

As a general rule, the more central to the mission of the company the violation is and the more people it affects, the more important it is that the apology be pitch-perfect. For core violations, the "what" has to show a tremendous commitment to change, the "who" has to be senior leaders, the "when" has to be fast, the "where" has to be high profile, and the "how" must be deeply sincere and demonstrate empathy.

There are some industries that apologize so frequently that they have the practice down to a science. Restaurants inevitably make mistakes—taking an order incorrectly, preparing the wrong dish, miscalculating the bill—and diners have come to expect a quick visit and an apology from the manager, along with a small offering (often a free dessert) as a consolation. When a Ritz-Carlton hotel failed to deliver a wake-up call at the appointed hour, causing a guest to run late for an important meeting, the front desk manager immediately apologized and offered to send up a complimentary breakfast. When the guest returned that evening, she found a handwritten apology from the general manager, fresh strawberries, dried fruit, and candy. Rather than lambaste the hotel, she raved to her friends about the five-star service she received.

It's imperative to give forethought to the kinds of events that will create the need for an organizational apology and how it will be executed. We recommend role-playing and "apology rehearsals." Making these investments is not strictly about damage control: A well-executed apology can improve relationships with customers, employees, and the public, leaving the company better positioned than it was before the error. That's an outcome to which every leader should aspire.

Originally published in September 2015. Reprint R1509B

What's Your Story?

by Herminia Ibarra and Kent Lineback

AT A RECENT NETWORKING EVENT, senior managers who'd been downsized out of high-paying corporate jobs took turns telling what they had done before and what they were looking for next. Person after person stood up and recounted a laundry list of credentials and jobs, in chronological order. Many felt compelled to begin with their first job, some even with their place of birth. The accounting was meticulous.

Most people spent their allotted two minutes (and lost the attention of those around them) before they even reached the punch line—the description of what they were seeking. Those who did leave time to wrap up tended merely to list the four or five (disparate) things they might be interested in pursuing next. In the feedback sessions that followed each round of presentations, these "fact tellers" were hard to help. The people listening couldn't readily understand how their knowledge and contacts might bear upon the teller's situation. Even worse, they didn't feel compelled to try very hard.

In our research and coaching on career reorientation, we've witnessed many people struggling to explain what they want to do next and why a change makes sense. One of us, in the context of writing a book, has studied a wide variety of major career shifts; the other has worked extensively with organizations and individuals on the use of narrative to bring about positive change. Each of us has been to enough networking events to know that the one we've described here is not unusual. But we've also seen a lot of people in the midst of significant transitions make effective use of contacts and successfully enlist supporters. What we've come to understand is that one factor more than any other makes the difference: the ability to craft a good story.

Why You Need a Story

All of us tell stories about ourselves. Stories define us. To know someone well is to know her story—the experiences that have shaped her, the trials and turning points that have tested her. When we want someone to know us, we share stories of our childhoods, our families, our school years, our first loves, the development of our political views, and so on.

Seldom is a good story so needed, though, as when a major change of professional direction is under way—when we are leaving A without yet having left it and moving toward B without yet having gotten there. In a time of such unsettling transition, telling a compelling story to coworkers, bosses, friends, or family—or strangers in a conference room—inspires belief in our motives, character, and capacity to reach the goals we've set.

Let's be clear: In urging the use of effective narrative, we're not opening the door to tall tales. By "story" we don't mean "something made up to make a bad situation look good." Rather, we're talking about accounts that are deeply true and so engaging that listeners feel they have a stake in our success. This dynamic was lacking in the event described above. Without a story, there was no context to render career facts meaningful, no promise of a third act in which achieving a goal (getting a job, for instance) would resolve the drama.

Creating and telling a story that resonates also helps us believe in ourselves. Most of us experience the transition to a new working life as a time of confusion, loss, insecurity, and uncertainty. We are scared. "Will I look back one day and think this was the best thing that ever happened?" we ask ourselves. "Or will I realize that this was the beginning of the end, that it was all downhill from here?" We oscillate between holding on to the past and

Idea in Brief

When you're in the midst of a major career change, telling stories about your professional self can inspire others' belief in your character and in your capacity to take a leap and land on your feet. It also can help you believe in yourself.

Unfortunately, most of us fail to use the power of storytelling in pursuit of our professional goals. Tales of transition are especially challenging. Not knowing how to reconcile the built-in discontinuities in our work lives, we often relay just the facts. We present ourselves as safe—and dull and unremarkable.

That's not a necessary compromise. A transition story has inherent dramatic appeal. The protagonist is you, and what's at stake is your career. Discontinuity and tension are part of the experience. If these elements are missing from your career story, the tale will fall flat.

To demonstrate stability and earn listeners' trust, emphasize continuity and causality—show that your past is related to the present, and convey that a solid future is in sight. If you can make your story of transition cohere, you will have gone far in convincing the listener—and reassuring yourself—that the change makes sense for you and is likely to bring success.

embracing the future. Why? We have lost the narrative thread of our professional life. Without a compelling story that lends meaning, unity, and purpose to our lives, we feel lost and rudderless. We need a good story to reassure us that our plans make sense—that, in moving on, we are not discarding everything we have worked so hard to accomplish and selfishly putting family and livelihood at risk. It will give us motivation and help us endure frustration, suffering, and hard work.

A good story, then, is essential for making a successful transition. Yet most of us—like those at the networking event—fail to use the power of storytelling in pursuit of our cause. Or, when we do craft a story, we do it badly. In part, this may be because many of us have forgotten how to tell stories. But even the best storytellers find tales of transition challenging, with their built-in problems and tensions. Not knowing how to resolve these conflicts, we retreat to telling "just the facts."

Your Story Has Inherent Drama

At first glance, it's not obvious why stories of transition should present any problems at all. Almost by definition, they contain the stuff of good narrative. (See the sidebar "Key Elements of a Classic Story.") The protagonist is you, of course, and what's at stake is your career. Only love, life, and death could be more important. And transition is always about a world that's changed. You've been let go, or you've somehow decided your life doesn't work anymore. Perhaps you've reached an event or insight that represents a point of no return—one that marks the end of the second act, a period of frustration and struggle. In the end, if all goes well, you resolve the tension and uncertainty and embark on a new chapter in your life or career.

Not only do transition stories have all the elements of a classic tale, but they have the most important ones in spades. Notice what moves a story along. It's change, conflict, tension, discontinuity. What hooks us in a movie or novel is the turning point, the break with the past, the fact that the world has changed in some intriguing and fascinating way that will force the protagonist to discover and reveal who he truly is. If those elements are missing, the story will be flat. It will lack what novelist John Gardner called profluence of development—the sense of moving forward, of going somewhere. Transition stories don't have this problem.

Think, for example, of the biblical story of Saint Paul's conversion. In his zeal for Jewish law, Saul had become a violent persecutor of Christians. On the road to Damascus, as the story is told in the New Testament, he was surrounded by light and struck to the ground. A voice from heaven addressed him: "Saul, Saul, why do you persecute me?" He was unable to see; after he changed his mind about Christians, he saw the light, literally. And thus, Saul became Paul, one of the principal architects of Christianity.

What could be more dramatic? Like the Saul-to-Paul saga, most after-the-fact accounts of career change include striking jolts and triggers: palpable moments when things click into place and a desirable option materializes. The scales fall from our eyes, and the right course becomes obvious—or taking the leap suddenly looks easy.

Here's how that turning point took shape for one manager, a 46-year-old information technologist named Lucy Hartman (names in the examples throughout this article have been changed). Lucy was seemingly on a course toward executive management, either at her current company or at a start-up. Being coached, however, revealed to her an attractive alternative. She began to wonder about a future as an organizational-development consultant, but she wasn't quite ready to make that change. She did move to a smaller company, where she felt she could apply everything she had learned in coaching. "By this time, it was clear that I wanted to move on to something different," she said. "But I needed to build more confidence before taking a bigger chance on reinventing myself. So I decided to stay in the high-tech environment, which I knew well, but also to go back to school. I started a master's program in organizational development, thinking it would at least make me a better leader and hoping it would be the impetus for a real makeover." Still, Lucy agonized for months over whether to focus exclusively on school, convinced that it wasn't sane to quit a job without having another one lined up.

Three incidents in quick succession made up her mind. First, she attended a conference on organizational change where she heard industry gurus speak and met other people working in the field. She decided this was clearly the community she wanted to be a part of. Second, her firm went through an acquisition, and the restructuring meant a new position for her, one fraught with political jockeying. Third, as she tells it: "One day my husband just asked me, 'Are you happy?' He said, 'If you are, that's great. But you don't look happy. When I ask how you are, all you ever say is that you're tired.'" His question prompted her to quit her job and work full-time on her master's.

Lucy's story illustrates the importance of turning points. We need them to convince ourselves that our story makes sense, and listeners like them because they spin stories off in exciting new directions. They make listeners lean forward and ask the one question every effective story must elicit: "What happened next?"

mini cliff hangers

Key Elements of a Classic Story

ALL GREAT STORIES, from *Antigone* to *Casablanca* to *Star Wars,* derive their power from several basic characteristics:

- **A protagonist the listener cares about.** The story must be about a person or group whose struggles we can relate to.

- **A catalyst compelling the protagonist to take action.** Somehow the world has changed so that something important is at stake. Typically, the first act of a play is devoted to establishing this fact. It's up to the protagonist to put things right again.

- **Trials and tribulations.** The story's second act commences as obstacles produce frustration, conflict, and drama, and often lead the protagonist to change in an essential way. As in *The Odyssey,* the trials reveal, test, and shape the protagonist's character. Time is spent wandering in the wilderness, far from home.

- **A turning point.** This represents a point of no return, which closes the second act. The protagonist can no longer see or do things the same way as before.

- **A resolution.** This is the third act, in which the protagonist either succeeds magnificently or fails tragically.

This is the classic beginning-middle-end story structure defined by Aristotle more than 2,300 years ago and used by countless others since. It seems to reflect how the human mind wants to organize reality.

The Challenge of the Transition Story

Let's return to that networking event and all the drab stories (actually, nonstories) people told. If transition stories, with their drama and discontinuity, lend themselves so well to vivid telling, why did so many people merely recount the basic facts of their careers and avoid the exciting turning points? Why did most of them try to frame the changes in their lives as incremental, logical extensions of what they were doing before? Why did they fail to play up the narrative twists and turns?

To begin with, it's because they were attempting to tell the story while they were still in the middle of the second act. Look back over Lucy's story, and you'll realize that the turning points she described were not very different from incidents all of us experience daily. They assumed great significance for Lucy only because she made them do so. For most of us, turning points are like Lucy's rather than Saul's; they tend to be much more obvious in the telling than in the living. We must learn to use them to propel our stories forward.

Additionally, stories of transition present a challenge because telling them well involves baring some emotion. You have to let the listener know that something is at stake for you personally. When you're in a job interview or when you are speaking to relative strangers, that is difficult to do.

Another issue that makes life stories (particularly ones about discontinuity) problematic: Not only does a good story require us to trust the listener, but it must also inspire the listener to trust us. A story about life discontinuity raises red flags about the teller's capabilities, dependability, and predictability. Listeners wonder, "Why should I believe you can excel in a new arena when you don't have a track record to point to?" And on a deeper level, even greater suspicions lurk: "Why should I trust that you won't change your mind about this? You changed your mind before, didn't you?"

To tell a life story that emphasizes such juicy elements as transformation and discontinuity is to invite questions about who we are and whether we can be trusted. No one wants to hire somebody who's likely to fly off in an unexpected direction every six months. So we downplay the very things that might make our stories compelling. To earn the listener's trust, we make ourselves appear safe—and dull and unremarkable.

Is there a way to tell a lively story *and* inspire others' confidence? Yes, but it requires a deep understanding of what really makes people believe in what we're saying.

The Struggle for Coherence

All good stories have a characteristic so basic and necessary it's often assumed. That quality is coherence, and it's crucial to life stories of transition.

This was a challenge for Sam Tierman, a former corporate HR executive one of us coached through a career transition. Sam had spent 18 years running HR in a number of good-sized regional banks, but his last three jobs hadn't ended well. He'd been downsized out of one, he'd quit another in frustration, and he'd been fired from the last—which finally led him to realize he had a career problem. While he was energized by the interplay between individuals and organizations, he hated the mundane, administrative aspects of the work. When he had a boss who considered HR a strategic function and who included the HR head at the executive table, he thrived. But when he worked for someone who saw HR as a body shop—"Find the bodies, run the benefits, and keep the government off our back"—Sam hated his work. In his last job, his feelings had been obvious, and a minor problem with some personnel analysis was what did him in. Sam, in fact, had taken this job with high hopes. The CEO who hired him considered HR strategic. Unfortunately, that CEO left and was replaced by one who did not.

As a result, Sam gave up on finding or keeping a boss he could work with in a corporate setting. As do so many frustrated executives, he decided he would prefer to work for a start-up. The problem was that he lacked, on the face of it, any of the experience or qualities wanted by people who found and fund start-ups. It was not obvious how Sam could tell a coherent career story that would bridge the chasm between stodgy overhead departments in banks and the high-energy world of start-ups.

Coherent narratives hang together in ways that feel natural and intuitive. A coherent life story is one that suggests what we all want to believe of ourselves and those we help or hire—that our lives are series of unfolding, linked events that make sense. In other words, the past is related to the present, and from that trajectory, we can glimpse our future.

Coherence is crucial to a life story of transition because it is the characteristic that most generates the listener's trust. If you can make your story of change and reinvention seem coherent, you will have gone far in convincing the listener that the change makes sense for you and is likely to bring success—and that you're a stable, trustworthy person.

As important, you will also have gone far in convincing yourself. Indeed, it's the loss of coherence that makes times of transition so difficult to get through. Think of the cartoon character who's run off the edge of a cliff. Legs still churning like crazy, he doesn't realize he's over the abyss—until he looks down. Each of us in transition feels like that character. Coherence is the solid ground under our feet. Without it, we feel as though we're hanging in midair—and we're afraid that if we look down, we'll plummet to our doom.

Charlotte Linde, a linguist who has studied the importance of coherence in life stories, makes clear in her work that coherence emerges in large part from continuity and causality. If we fail to observe these two principles, we create a sense of incoherence, or, in Linde's words, the "chilling possibility that one's life is random, accidental, unmotivated." And what's chilling to us will certainly be off-putting to those listening to our stories.

Emphasizing Continuity and Causality

Now it becomes understandable why so many speakers in that networking meeting failed to do more than recite facts. They were trying to downplay discontinuity; to gloss over how large a professional jump they wanted to make; to avoid appearing wayward, lost, and flailing. It was a misguided strategy, for listeners are particularly sensitive to lapses of coherence in life stories. They actually *look for* coherence in such stories. Failure to acknowledge a large degree of change will put off listeners and undermine their trust.

As storytellers, we must deal explicitly with the magnitude of change our stories communicate. We can do that and still inspire trust if we focus on establishing continuity and causality. The following suggestions can help.

Keep your reasons for change grounded in your character, in who you are

There's probably no rationale for change more compelling than some internal reason, some basic character trait. In its simplest version, this explanation takes the form of "I discovered I'm good at

Does Your Résumé Tell a Story?

Though the terms are often used interchangeably, there's a big difference between a curriculum vitae and a résumé.

A CV is an exhaustive and strictly chronological list of facts about your professional life. You may need one, but don't expect it to serve your cause in a period of transition. To the extent it tells a story, that story is constructed wholly in the reader's mind.

If you want to give your credentials narrative shape, use a résumé—and understand that you will almost certainly need more than one version. Each will highlight and interpret your experience differently in light of the job or career alternatives you're exploring.

The process of putting together a résumé is as valuable as the product, because it entails drafting your story. Everything in the résumé must point to one goal—which, of course, is the climax of the story you're telling. Build it in three parts.

First, describe the position you want.

---

that" or "I like that—it gives me real pleasure." This approach, noted by Linde and found by us in our work to be extremely useful, allows storytellers to incorporate learning and self-discovery into life stories. We can try something, learn from the experience, and use that learning to deepen our understanding of what we want. Many turning points can be used in this way. Note that it's not wise to base the reasons for transformation primarily outside ourselves. "I got fired" may be a fact we must explain and incorporate into our stories, but it's rarely recognized as a good justification for seeking whatever we're seeking. External reasons tend to create the impression that we simply accept our fate.

Cite multiple reasons for what you want
You might, for instance, mention both personal and professional grounds for making a change. (Obviously, these must be complementary rather than mutually exclusive or contradictory.) The richer and more varied the reasons compelling you to change, the more comprehensible and acceptable that change will appear. Sam, the former HR executive, was able to cite a number of unusual projects

Second, create a bulleted list of experience highlights that clearly demonstrate your ability to do that job. Consider every piece of experience you have (don't forget volunteer work or anything else that might apply), and identify which parts support the story you're telling.

Third, summarize your professional work. This section of your résumé has the appearance of a CV, in reverse chronological order, and includes all the relevant positions you've held; for each job, it shows dates of employment as well as your responsibilities and accomplishments. But these descriptions are couched in the same terms as your experience highlights. In fact, every claim in your highlights section (which supports your overall goal) must be supported by your job summaries.

Follow these steps, and your résumé will tell a coherent story. The work you have done, and the skills and interests you have developed and revealed, will point to a clear and desirable resolution: your stated goal.

he had worked on, which indicated, though in a big-company context, his ability to think and act entrepreneurially. Additionally, his undergraduate training in electrical engineering and his MBA in finance from a prestigious school were evidence of the technical and analytical bent preferred by the start-ups he knew.

Be sure to point out any explanations that extend back in time
A goal rooted in the past will serve far better than one recently conceived. Your story will need to show why you could not pursue the goal originally, but here, external causes—illness, accident, family problems, being drafted, and so on—can play a leading role.

Reframe your past in light of the change you're seeking to make
This is not to suggest that you hide anything or prevaricate. We all continually rethink and retell our own life stories. We create different versions that focus on or downplay, include or exclude, different aspects of what has happened to us. Some elements of the jobs we've held probably fit well with our change plans and can be used to link our past experiences with the part of our life that we're advancing

toward. The key is to dissect those experiences and find the pieces that relate to our current goals. (For advice on how to do this, see the sidebar "Does Your Résumé Tell a Story?")

Choose a story form that lends itself to your tale of reinvention
Certain forms—love stories, war stories, epics—are as old as narrative itself. There are stories of being tested and stories of being punished. When it comes to describing transition and reinvention, it can be helpful to present the story in a vessel familiar to most listeners. Of the time-honored approaches, two to consider are the maturation (or coming-of-age) plot and the education plot.

The maturation plot was useful to Gary McCarthy, who quit his job as a strategy consultant with no idea of what he would do next. As he told his story at age 35, he looked back over his career and realized he had always responded to social pressure, bending to what others thought was the right thing for him to do. After receiving a negative performance appraisal, he saw that he needed to be his own man. "You'd better be damn sure when you wake up that you're doing what you want to be doing," he said to himself, "as opposed to what you feel you ought to be doing or what somebody else thinks you ought to be doing."

Lucy Hartman's story is a good example of the education plot, which recounts change generated by growing insight and self-understanding. It was a mentor, her executive coach, who let her glimpse a possible new future, and she continued to learn in her master's program and by coaching others. In her version of events, the more she learned about the human side of enterprise, the more she realized her desire to work in and contribute to this area.

All these suggestions are ways to frame the discontinuity in a transition story and provide the coherence that will reassure listeners. They demonstrate that, at your core, the person you were yesterday is the person you are today and the person you will be tomorrow. And they establish that there are good and sufficient causes for change. If you create the sense that your life hangs (and will hang) together, you'll be free to incorporate the dramatic elements of change and turmoil and uncertainty into your story that will make it compelling.

Telling Multiple Stories

We've noted the challenge of crafting a story, complete with dramatic turning points, when the outcome is still far from clear. The truth is, as you embark on a career transition, you will likely find yourself torn among different interests, paths, and priorities. It wouldn't be unusual, for example, for you to work all weekend on a business plan for a start-up, return to your day job on Monday and ask for a transfer to another position or business unit, and then have lunch on Tuesday with a headhunter to explore yet a third option. This is simply the nature of career transition. So how do you reconcile this reality with the need to present a clear, single life story of reinvention, one that implies you know exactly where you're going?

For starters, keep in mind that, in a job interview, you don't establish trust by getting everything off your chest or being completely open about the several possibilities you are exploring. In the early stages of a transition, it is important to identify and actively consider multiple alternatives. But you will explore each option, or type of option, with a different audience.

This means that you must craft different stories for different possible selves (and the various audiences that relate to those selves). Sam chose to focus on start-ups as the result of a process that began with examining his own experience. He realized that he had felt most alive during times he described as "big change fast"—a bankruptcy, a turnaround, and a rapid reorganization. So he developed three stories to support his goal of building a work life around "big change fast": one about the HR contributions he could make on a team at a consulting company that specialized in taking clients through rapid change; one about working for a firm that bought troubled companies and rapidly turned them around; and one about working for a start-up, probably a venture between its first and second, or second and third, rounds of financing. He tested these stories on friends and at networking events and eventually wrangled referrals and job interviews for each kind of job.

The process is not only about keeping options open as long as possible; it's also about learning which ones to pursue most energetically. In Sam's case, what became clear over a number of conversations was that the consulting firms he respected tended not to hire people of his age and credentials unless they had perfectly relevant experience. Neither did opportunities with turnaround firms appear to be panning out. But Sam did make progress toward some start-ups. After one of them engaged him for a series of consulting assignments, he was able to convert that relationship into a job as chief administrative officer. That position, in turn, exposed him to many contacts in the start-up community. Most important, it stamped him as a bona fide member of that world. Having stripped the stodgy corporate aura from his résumé, he eventually became the CEO of a start-up set to commercialize some technology developed by and spun out of a large company. By this point, four full years had elapsed, and Sam had revised his narrative many times, with each step contributing to a more and more coherent story of change.

Just Tell It

Any veteran storyteller will agree that there's no substitute for practicing in front of a live audience. Tell and retell your story; rework it like a draft of an epic novel until the "right" version emerges.

You can practice your stories in many ways and places. Any context will do in which you're likely to be asked, "What can you tell me about yourself?" or "What do you do?" or "What are you looking for?" Start with family and friends. You may even want to designate a small circle of friends and close colleagues, with their knowledge and approval, your "board of advisers." Their primary function would be to listen and react again and again to your evolving stories. Many of the people we have studied or coached through the transition process have created or joined networking groups for just this purpose.

You'll know you've honed your story when it feels both comfortable and true to you. But you cannot get there until you put yourself in front of others—ultimately, in front of strangers—and watch their faces and body language as you speak. For one woman we know,

June Prescott, it was not simply that practice made for polished presentation—although her early efforts to explain herself were provisional, even clumsy. (She was attempting a big career change, from academe to Wall Street.) Each time she wrote a cover letter, interviewed, or updated friends and family on her progress, she better defined what was exciting to her; and in each public declaration of her intent to change careers, she committed herself further.

June's experience teaches a final, important lesson about undergoing change. We use stories to reinvent ourselves. June, like Sam, was able to change because she created a story that justified and motivated such a dramatic shift.

This is the role of storytelling in times of personal transition. Getting the story right is critical, as much for motivating ourselves as for enlisting the help of others. Anyone trying to make a change has to work out a story that connects the old and new selves. For it is in a period of change that we often fail, yet most need, to link our past, present, and future into a compelling whole.

Originally published in January 2005. Reprint R0501F

Visualizations That Really Work

by Scott Berinato

NOT LONG AGO, THE ABILITY to create smart data visualizations, or dataviz, was a nice-to-have skill. For the most part, it benefited design- and data-minded managers who made a deliberate decision to invest in acquiring it. That's changed. Now visual communication is a must-have skill for all managers, because more and more often, it's the only way to make sense of the work they do.

Data is the primary force behind this shift. Decision making increasingly relies on data, which comes at us with such overwhelming velocity, and in such volume, that we can't comprehend it without some layer of abstraction, such as a visual one. A typical example: At Boeing the managers of the Osprey program need to improve the efficiency of the aircraft's takeoffs and landings. But each time the Osprey gets off the ground or touches back down, its sensors create a terabyte of data. Ten takeoffs and landings produce as much data as is held in the Library of Congress. Without visualization, detecting the inefficiencies hidden in the patterns and anomalies of that data would be an impossible slog.

But even information that's not statistical demands visual expression. Complex systems—business process workflows, for example, or the way customers move through a store—are hard to understand, much less fix, if you can't first see them.

Thanks to the internet and a growing number of affordable tools, translating information into visuals is now easy (and cheap) for everyone, regardless of data skills or design skills. This is largely a positive development. One drawback, though, is that it reinforces the impulse to "click and viz" without first thinking about your purpose and goals. *Convenient* is a tempting replacement for good, but it will lead to charts that are merely adequate or, worse, ineffective. Automatically converting spreadsheet cells into a chart only visualizes pieces of a spreadsheet; it doesn't capture an idea. As the presentation expert Nancy Duarte puts it, "Don't project the idea that you're showing a chart. Project the idea that you're showing a reflection of human activity, of things people did to make a line go up and down. It's not 'Here are our Q3 financial results,' it's 'Here's where we missed our targets.'"

Managers who want to get better at making charts often start by learning rules. When should I use a bar chart? How many colors are too many? Where should the key go? Do I have to start my y-axis at zero? Visual grammar is important and useful—but knowing it doesn't guarantee that you'll make good charts. To start with chart-making rules is to forgo strategy for execution; it's to pack for a trip without knowing where you're going.

Your visual communication will prove far more successful if you begin by acknowledging that it is not a lone action but, rather, several activities, each of which requires distinct types of planning, resources, and skills. The typology I offer here was created as a reaction to my making the very mistake I just described: The book from which this article is adapted started out as something like a rule book. But after exploring the history of visualization, the exciting state of visualization research, and smart ideas from experts and pioneers, I reconsidered the project. We didn't need another rule book; we needed a way to think about the increasingly crucial discipline of visual communication as a whole.

The typology described in this article is simple. By answering just two questions, you can set yourself up to succeed.

The Two Questions

To start thinking visually, consider the nature and purpose of your visualization:

Idea in Brief

Context

Knowledge workers need greater visual literacy than they used to, because so much data—and so many ideas—are now presented graphically. But few of us have been taught data-visualization skills.

Tools Are Fine . . .

Inexpensive tools allow anyone to perform simple tasks such as importing spreadsheet data into a bar chart. But that means it's easy to create terrible charts. Visualization can be so much more: It's an agile, powerful way to explore ideas and communicate information.

. . . But Strategy Is Key

Don't jump straight to execution. Instead, first think about what you're representing—ideas or data? Then consider your purpose: Do you want to inform, persuade, or explore? The answers will suggest what tools and resources you need.

Is the information *conceptual* or *data-driven?*

Am I *declaring* something or *exploring* something?

If you know the answers to these questions, you can plan what resources and tools you'll need and begin to discern what type of visualization will help you achieve your goals most effectively.

	Conceptual	Data-driven
Focus	*Ideas*	*Statistics*
Goals	*Simplify, teach* "Here's how our organization is structured."	*Inform, enlighten* "Here are our revenues for the past two years."

The first question is the simpler of the two, and the answer is usually obvious. Either you're visualizing qualitative information or you're plotting quantitative information: ideas or statistics. But notice that the question is about the information itself, not the forms you might ultimately use to show it. For example, the classic Gartner Hype Cycle (see following page) uses a traditionally data-driven form—a line chart—but no actual data. It's a concept.

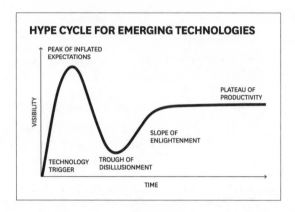

If the first question identifies what you *have*, the second elicits what you're *doing*: either communicating information (declarative) or trying to figure something out (exploratory).

	Declarative	Exploratory
Focus	*Documenting, designing*	*Prototyping, iterating, interacting, automating*
Goals	*Affirm* "Here is our budget by department."	*Confirm* "Let's see if marketing investments contributed to rising profits." *Discover* "What would we see if we visualized customer purchases by gender, location, and purchase amount in real time?"

Managers most often work with declarative visualizations, which make a statement, usually to an audience in a formal setting. If you have a spreadsheet workbook full of sales data and you're using it to show quarterly sales in a presentation, your purpose is declarative.

But let's say your boss wants to understand why the sales team's performance has lagged lately. You suspect that seasonal cycles have caused the dip, but you're not sure. Now your purpose is exploratory, and you'll use the same data to create visuals that will confirm or refute your hypothesis. The audience is usually yourself or a small team. If your hypothesis is confirmed, you may well show your boss a declarative visualization, saying, "Here's what's happening to sales."

Exploratory visualizations are actually of two kinds. In the example above, you were testing a hypothesis. But suppose you don't have an idea about why performance is lagging—you don't know what you're looking for. You want to mine your workbook to see what patterns, trends, and anomalies emerge. What will you see, for example, when you measure sales performance in relation to the size of the region a salesperson manages? What happens if you compare seasonal trends in various geographies? How does weather affect sales? Such data brainstorming can deliver fresh insights. Big strategic questions—Why are revenues falling? Where can we find efficiencies? How do customers interact with us?—can benefit from a discovery-focused exploratory visualization.

The Four Types

The nature and purpose questions combine in a classic 2×2 to define four types of visual communication: idea illustration, idea generation, visual discovery, and everyday dataviz.

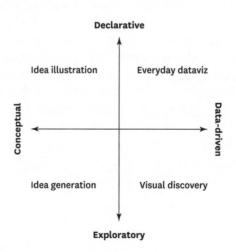

Idea illustration

Info type	Process, framework
Typical setting	Presentations, teaching
Primary skills	Design, editing
Goals	Learning, simplifying, explaining

We might call this quadrant the "consultants' corner." Consultants can't resist process diagrams, cycle diagrams, and the like. At their best, idea illustrations clarify complex ideas by drawing on our ability to understand metaphors (trees, bridges) and simple design conventions (circles, hierarchies). Org charts and decision trees are classic examples of idea illustration. So is the 2×2 that frames this article.

Idea illustration demands clear and simple design, but its reliance on metaphor invites unnecessary adornment. Because the discipline and boundaries of data sets aren't built in to idea illustration, they must be imposed. The focus should be on clear communication, structure, and the logic of the ideas. The most useful skills here are similar to what a text editor brings to a manuscript—the ability to pare things down to their essence. Some design skills will be useful too, whether they're your own or hired.

Suppose a company engages consultants to help its R&D group find inspiration in other industries. The consultants use a technique called the *pyramid search*—a way to get information from experts in other fields close to your own, who point you to the top experts in their fields, who point you to experts in still other fields, who then help you find the experts in those fields, and so on.

It's actually tricky to explain, so the consultants may use visualization to help. How does a pyramid search work? It looks something like this:

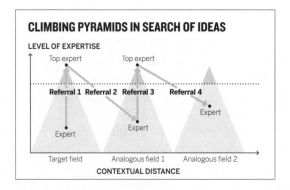

The axes use conventions that we can grasp immediately: industries plotted near to far and expertise mapped low to high. The pyramid shape itself shows the relative rarity of top experts compared with lower-level ones. Words in the title—"climbing" and "pyramids"—help us grasp the idea quickly. Finally, the designer didn't succumb to a temptation to decorate: The pyramids aren't literal, three-dimensional, sandstone-colored objects.

Too often, idea illustration doesn't go that well, and you end up with something like this:

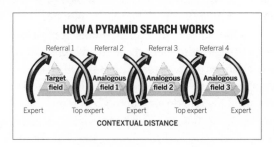

Here the color gradient, the drop shadows, and the 3-D pyramids distract us from the idea. The arrows don't actually demonstrate how a pyramid search works. And experts and top experts are placed on the same plane instead of at different heights to convey relative status.

Idea generation

Info type	Complex, undefined
Typical setting	Working session, brainstorming
Primary skills	Team-building, facilitation
Goals	Problem solving, discovery, innovation

Managers may not think of visualization as a tool to support idea generation, but they use it to brainstorm all the time—on white-boards, on butcher paper, or, classically, on the back of a napkin. Like idea illustration, idea generation relies on conceptual meta-phors, but it takes place in more-informal settings, such as off-sites, strategy sessions, and early-phase innovation projects. It's used to find new ways of seeing how the business works and to answer complex managerial challenges: restructuring an organization, coming up with a new business process, codifying a system for making decisions.

Although idea generation can be done alone, it benefits from collaboration and borrows from design thinking—gathering as many diverse points of view and visual approaches as possible before homing in on one and refining it. Jon Kolko, the founder and director of the Austin Center for Design and the author of *Well-Designed: How to Use Empathy to Create Products People Love,* fills the whiteboard walls of his office with conceptual, exploratory visualizations. "It's our go-to method for thinking through complexity," he says. "Sketching is this effort to work through ambiguity and muddiness and come to crispness." Managers who are good at leading teams, facilitating brainstorming sessions, and encouraging and then capturing creative thinking will do well in this quadrant. Design skills and editing are less important here, and sometimes counterproductive. When you're seeking breakthroughs, editing is the opposite of what you need, and you should think in rapid sketches; refined designs will just slow you down.

Suppose a marketing team is holding an off-site. The team members need to come up with a way to show executives their proposed strategy for going upmarket. An hour-long whiteboard session yields several approaches and ideas (none of which are erased) for presenting the strategy. Ultimately, one approach gains purchase with the team, which thinks it best captures the key point: Get fewer customers to spend much more. The whiteboard looks something like this:

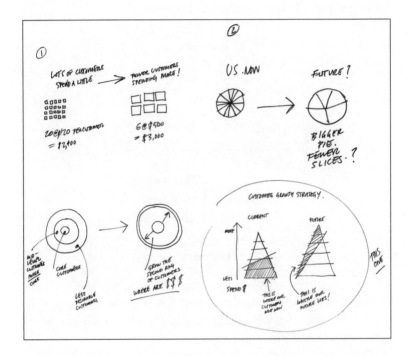

Of course, visuals that emerge from idea generation often lead to more formally designed and presented idea illustrations.

Visual discovery

Info type	Big data, complex, dynamic
Typical setting	Working sessions, testing, analysis
Primary skills	Business intelligence, programming, paired analysis
Goals	Trend spotting, sense making, deep analysis

This is the most complicated quadrant, because in truth it holds two categories. Recall that we originally separated exploratory purposes into two kinds: testing a hypothesis and mining for patterns, trends, and anomalies. The former is focused, whereas the latter is more flexible. The bigger and more complex the data, and the less you know going in, the more open-ended the work.

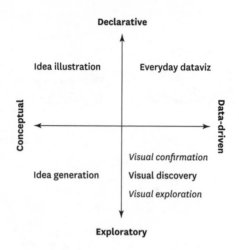

Visual confirmation. You're answering one of two questions with this kind of project: Is what I suspect actually true? or What are some other ways of depicting this idea?

The scope of the data tends to be manageable, and the chart types you're likely to use are common—although when trying to depict things in new ways, you may venture into some less-common types. Confirmation usually doesn't happen in a formal setting; it's the work you do to find the charts you want to create for presentations. That means your time will shift away from design and toward proto-typing that allows you to rapidly iterate on the dataviz. Some skill at manipulating spreadsheets and knowledge of programs or sites that enable swift prototyping are useful here.

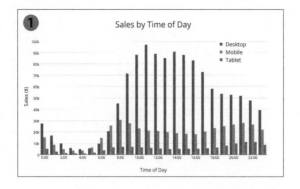

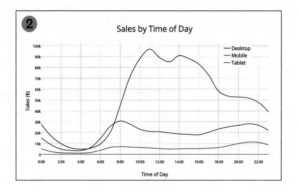

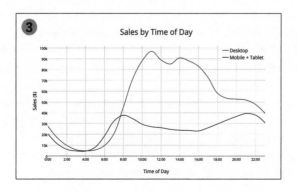

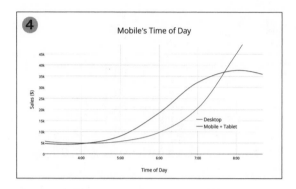

Suppose a marketing manager believes that at certain times of the day more customers shop his site on mobile devices than on desktops, but his marketing programs aren't designed to take advantage of that. He loads some data into an online tool (called Datawrapper) to see if he's right (1 on previous page).

He can't yet confirm or refute his hypothesis. He can't tell much of anything, but he's prototyping and using a tool that makes it easy to try different views into the data. He works fast; design is not a concern. He tries a line chart instead of a bar chart (2).

Now he's seeing something, but working with three variables still doesn't quite get at the mobile-versus-desktop view he wants, so he tries again with two variables (3). Each time he iterates, he evaluates whether he can confirm his original hypothesis: At certain times of day more customers are shopping on mobile devices than on desktops.

On the fourth try he zooms in and confirms his hypothesis (4).

New software tools mean this type of visualization is easier than ever before: They're making data analysts of us all.

Visual exploration. Open-ended data-driven visualizations tend to be the province of data scientists and business intelligence analysts, although new tools have begun to engage general managers in visual exploration. It's exciting to try, because it often produces insights that can't be gleaned any other way.

Because we don't know what we're looking for, these visuals tend to plot data more inclusively. In extreme cases, this kind of project may combine multiple data sets or load dynamic, real-time data into a system that updates automatically. Statistical modeling benefits from visual exploration.

Exploration also lends itself to interactivity: Managers can adjust parameters, inject new data sources, and continually revisualize. Complex data sometimes also suits specialized and unusual visualization, such as *force-directed diagrams* that show how networks cluster, or topographical plots.

Function trumps form here: Analytical, programming, data management, and business intelligence skills are more crucial than the ability to create presentable charts. Not surprisingly, this half of the quadrant is where managers are most likely to call in experts to help set up systems to wrangle data and create visualizations that fit their analytic goals.

Anmol Garg, a data scientist at Tesla Motors, has used visual exploration to tap into the vast amount of sensor data the company's cars produce. Garg created an interactive chart that shows the pressure in a car's tires over time. In true exploratory form, he and his team first created the visualizations and then found a variety of uses for them: to see whether tires are properly inflated when a car leaves the factory, how often customers reinflate them, and how long customers take to respond to a low-pressure alert; to find leak rates; and to do some predictive modeling on when tires are likely to go flat. The pressure of all four tires is visualized on a scatter plot, which, however inscrutable to a general audience, is clear to its intended audience.

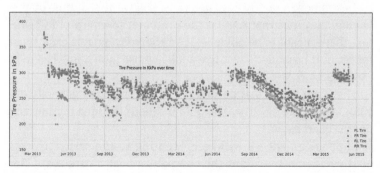

Garg was exploring data to find insights that could be gleaned only through visuals. "We're dealing with terabytes of data all the time," he says. "You can't find anything looking at spreadsheets and querying databases. It has to be visual." For presentations to the executive team, Garg translates these exploration sessions into the kinds of simpler charts discussed below. "Management loves seeing visualizations," he says.

Everyday dataviz

Info type	Simple, low volume
Typical setting	Formal, presentations
Primary skills	Design, storytelling
Goals	Affirming, setting context

Whereas data scientists do most of the work on visual exploration, managers do most of the work on everyday visualizations. This quadrant comprises the basic charts and graphs you normally paste from a spreadsheet into a presentation. They are usually simple—line charts, bar charts, pies, and scatter plots.

"Simple" is the key. Ideally, the visualization will communicate a single message, charting only a few variables. And the goal is straightforward: affirming and setting context. Simplicity is primarily a design challenge, so design skills are important. Clarity and consistency make these charts most effective in the setting where they're typically used: a formal presentation. In a presentation, time is constrained. A poorly designed chart will waste that time by provoking questions that require the presenter to interpret information that's meant to be obvious. If an everyday dataviz can't speak for itself, it has failed—just like a joke whose punch line has to be explained.

That's not to say that declarative charts shouldn't generate discussion. But the discussion should be about the idea in the chart, not the chart itself.

Suppose an HR VP will be presenting to the rest of the executive committee about the company's health care costs. She wants to convey that the growth of these costs has slowed significantly, creating an opportunity to invest in additional health care services.

The VP has read an online report about this trend that includes a link to some government data. She downloads the data and clicks on the line chart option in Excel. She has her viz in a few seconds. But because this is for a presentation, she asks a designer colleague to add detail from the data set to give a more comprehensive view.

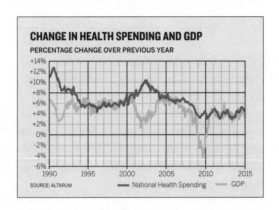

CHANGE IN HEALTH SPENDING AND GDP
PERCENTAGE CHANGE OVER PREVIOUS YEAR

SOURCE: ALTARUM ▬ National Health Spending ▬ GDP

This is a well-designed, accurate chart, but it's probably not the right one. The executive committee doesn't need two decades' worth of historical context to discuss the company's strategy for employee benefits investments. The point the VP wants to make is that cost increases have slowed over the past few years. Is that clearly communicated here?

In general, when it takes more than a few seconds to digest the data in a chart, the chart will work better on paper or on a personal-device screen, for someone who's not expected to listen to a presentation while trying to take in so much information. For example, health care policy makers might benefit from seeing this chart in advance of a hearing at which they'll discuss these long-term trends.

Our VP needs something cleaner for her context. She could make her point as simply as this:

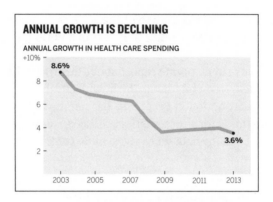

ANNUAL GROWTH IS DECLINING

ANNUAL GROWTH IN HEALTH CARE SPENDING

Simplicity like this takes some discipline—and courage—to achieve. The impulse is to include everything you know. Busy charts communicate the idea that you've been just that—busy. "Look at all the data I have and the work I've done," they seem to say. But that's not the VP's goal. She wants to persuade her colleagues to invest in new programs. With this chart, she won't have to utter a word for the executive team to understand the trend. She has clearly established a foundation for her recommendations.

In some ways, "data visualization" is a terrible term. It seems to reduce the construction of good charts to a mechanical procedure. It evokes the tools and methodology required to create rather than the creation itself. It's like calling *Moby-Dick* a "word sequentialization" or *The Starry Night* a "pigment distribution."

It also reflects an ongoing obsession in the dataviz world with process over outcomes. Visualization is merely a process. What we actually do when we make a good chart is get at some truth and move people to feel it—to see what couldn't be seen before. To change minds. To cause action.

Some basic common grammar will improve our ability to communicate visually. But good outcomes require a broader understanding and a strategic approach—which the typology described here is meant to help you develop.

Originally published June 2016. Reprint R1606H

Structure Your Presentation Like a Story

by Nancy Duarte

AFTER STUDYING HUNDREDS OF SPEECHES, I've found that the most effective presenters use the same techniques as great storytellers: By reminding people of the status quo and then revealing the path to a better way, they set up a conflict that needs to be resolved.

That tension helps them persuade the audience to adopt a new mindset or behave differently—to move from what is to what could be. And by following Aristotle's three-part story structure (beginning, middle, end), they create a message that's easy to digest, remember, and retell. Here's how it looks when you chart it out:

Persuasive story pattern

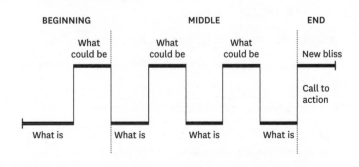

And here's how to use the persuasive story pattern in your own presentations.

Craft the Beginning

Start by describing life as the audience knows it. People should be nodding their heads in recognition because you're articulating what they already understand. This creates a bond between you and them, and opens them up to hear your ideas for change.

After you set that baseline of what is, introduce your vision of what could be. The gap between the two will throw the audience a bit off balance, and that's a good thing—it jars them out of complacency. For instance:

- *What is:* We fell short of our Q3 financial goals partly because we're understaffed and everyone's spread too thin.

- *What could be:* But what if we could solve the worst of our problems by bringing in a couple of powerhouse clients? Well, we can.

Once you establish that gap, use the rest of the presentation to bridge it

Develop the Middle

Now that people in your audience realize their world is off-kilter, keep playing up the contrast between what is and what could be.

Let's go back to that Q3 update. Revenues are down, but you want to motivate employees to make up for it. Here's one way you could structure the middle of your presentation:

- *What is:* We missed our Q3 forecast by 15%.

- *What could be:* Q4 numbers must be strong for us to pay out bonuses.

- *What is:* We have six new clients on our roster.

- *What could be:* Two of them have the potential to bring in more revenue than our best clients do now.

- *What is:* The new clients will require extensive retooling in manufacturing.

- *What could be:* We'll be bringing in experts from Germany to help.

As you move back and forth between what is and what could be, the audience will find the latter more and more alluring.

Make the Ending Powerful

You don't want to end with a burdensome list of to-dos. Definitely include a call to action—but make it inspiring so people will want to act. Describe what I call the new bliss: how much better their world will be when they adopt your ideas.

So if you're wrapping up that Q3 update from above, you might approach it this way:

- *Call to action:* It will take extra work from all departments to make Q4 numbers, but we can deliver products to our important new clients on time and with no errors.

- *New bliss:* I know everyone's running on fumes—but hang in there. This is our chance to pull together like a championship team, and things will get easier if we make this work. The reward if we meet our Q4 targets? Bonuses, plus days off at the end of the year.

By defining future rewards, you show people that getting on board will be worth their effort. It'll meet their needs, not just yours.

Adapted from *HBR Guide to Persuasive Presentations*. Reprint H009MI

CHRIS ANDERSON is the curator of TED.

SUSAN J. ASHFORD is the Michael and Susan Jandernoa Professor of Management and Organizations at the University of Michigan's Ross School of Business.

SCOTT BERINATO is a senior editor at Harvard Business Review Press and the author of *Good Charts Workbook* (Harvard Business Review Press, 2019) and *Good Charts* (Harvard Business Review Press, 2016).

ALISON WOOD BROOKS is an assistant professor of business administration at Harvard Business School.

JAY A. CONGER is the Henry R. Kravis Research Chair in Leadership Studies at Claremont McKenna College.

AMY J.C. CUDDY is an associate professor of business administration at Harvard Business School.

JAMES R. DETERT is a professor of business administration and the associate dean of Executive Degree Programs and Leadership Initiatives at the University of Virginia's Darden School of Business.

NANCY DUARTE is a bestselling author with thirty years of CEO-ing under her belt. She's driven her firm, Duarte, Inc., to be the global leader behind some of the most influential messages and visuals in business and culture. Duarte, Inc., is the largest design firm in Silicon Valley, as well as one of the top woman-owned businesses in the area. Nancy has written six bestselling books, four have won awards, and her new book, *DataStory*, is available now.

BRONWYN FRYER is a contributing editor to hbr.org.

ADAM D. GALINSKY is the chair of the Management Division at Columbia Business School. He coauthored the critically acclaimed and bestselling book *Friend & Foe* (Crown Business, 2015) and produced a popular TED talk, "How to Speak Up for Yourself."

HERMINIA IBARRA is the Charles Handy Professor of Organizational Behavior at London Business School. Prior to joining LBS, she served on the INSEAD and Harvard Business School faculties. She is the author of *Act Like a Leader, Think Like a Leader* (Harvard Business Review Press, 2015) and *Working Identity* (Harvard Business Review Press, 2003).

MATTHEW KOHUT is a coauthor of *Compelling People* (Hudson Street Press, 2013) and a principal at KNP Communications.

KENT LINEBACK spent many years as a manager and an executive in business and government. He is a coauthor of *Collective Genius* (Harvard Business Review Press, 2014).

DANIEL McGINN is a senior editor at *Harvard Business Review* and the author of *Psyched Up* (Portfolio, 2017).

ROBERT McKEE is an author, lecturer, and story consultant who is widely known for his popular "Story Seminar," which he developed when he was a professor at the University of Southern California. He is the author of *Story* (ReganBooks, 1997), *Dialogue* (Twelve, 2016), and *Storynomics* (Twelve, 2018).

NICK MORGAN is a speaker, coach, and the president and founder of Public Words, a communications consulting firm. He is the author of *Power Cues* (Harvard Business Review Press, 2014).

JOHN NEFFINGER is a coauthor of *Compelling People* (Hudson Street Press, 2013) and a principal at KNP Communications.

MAURICE E. SCHWEITZER is the Cecilia Yen Koo Professor at the University of Pennsylvania's Wharton School. He and Adam D. Galinsky are the coauthors of *Friend & Foe* (Crown Business, 2015).

Index

Engage with HBR content the way you want, on any device.

With HBR's new subscription plans, you can access world-renowned **case studies** from Harvard Business School and receive **four free eBooks**. Download and customize prebuilt **slide decks and graphics** from our **Visual Library**. With HBR's archive, top 50 best-selling articles, and five new articles every day, HBR is more than just a magazine.

Subscribe Today
hbr.org/success

The most important management ideas all in one place.

We hope you enjoyed this book from *Harvard Business Review*. Now you can get even more with HBR's 10 Must Reads Boxed Set. From books on leadership and strategy to managing yourself and others, this 6-book collection delivers articles on the most essential business topics to help you succeed.

HBR's 10 Must Reads Series

The definitive collection of ideas and best practices on our most sought-after topics from the best minds in business.

- Change Management
- Collaboration
- Communication
- Emotional Intelligence
- Innovation
- Leadership
- Making Smart Decisions

- Managing Across Cultures
- Managing People
- Managing Yourself
- Strategic Marketing
- Strategy
- Teams
- The Essentials

hbr.org/mustreads

Buy for your team, clients, or event.
Visit hbr.org/bulksales for quantity discount rates.